The Case for
East Roman Studies

PAST IMPERFECT

Further Information and Publications
www.arc-humanities.org/our-series/pi

The Case for East Roman Studies

Anthony Kaldellis

ARCHUMANITIES PRESS

British Library Cataloguing in Publication Data

A catalogue record for this book is available from the British Library.

© 2024, Arc Humanities Press, Leeds

ISBN (print) 9781802701821
e-ISBN (PDF) 9781802702545
e-ISBN (EPUB) 9781802702552

www.arc-humanities.org

Printed and bound in the UK (by CPI Group [UK] Ltd), USA (by Bookmasters), and elsewhere using print-on-demand technology.

Contents

Introduction 1

Chapter 1. RIP Byzantium 9

Chapter 2. Contenders for a New Field-Name 25

Chapter 3. Implications for Allied Fields 63

Conclusions 99

Further Reading 103

Introduction

Byzantine Studies is at a tipping point, and it has come upon us suddenly, or at least it feels that way. At many recent conferences, colleagues either refuse to refer to "Byzantium" and "the Byzantines," or self-consciously place those terms within verbal quotation marks. There is a growing awareness not only that these terms are artificial, but that they distort the society which they purport to name and, moreover, that they originate in ideologies of western supremacy that we oppose in all other contexts. More than just a terminological problem, these words are emblematic of the deeper set of prejudices that have plagued our field since its inception. A range of negative associations have accrued in western imagination around "Byzantium," and the field has had to wage a never-ending battle to de-weed itself from them. This is not, then, just a problem of the "identity" of our subjects—though that is serious enough—but of the larger framework in which the east Roman empire is studied. Traditionally, Byzantine Studies has been a notoriously conservative field and averse to self-critique, but now many, especially younger, scholars are calling for a paradigm-shift. Leonora Neville has pointedly captured this predicament by referring at conferences to "the B-word."

It may feel as if these calls have crept up on us suddenly, but in reality we have reached this point through research that has accumulated gradually over the years, nudging us toward a realization that the field-name under which we labor unduly distorts the society that we study and places our field as a whole at a disadvantage. It has been a gradual process for me too. In graduate school, we all knew that the label "Byzantium" was a modern artifice but believed that it could serve as a neutral field-label for a society that we all knew was, and called itself, the Roman empire, a direct continuation of the ancient Roman empire in the east. Actually, even that is misleading, for there is no word in medieval Greek that means "empire." The terms actually used in the sources translate as "polity of the Romans," "monarchy of the Romans," or "state of the Romans." Wholly missing from the scholarship, however, was the proper name of this society, though it is amply attested in the sources: *Romanía*, which translates roughly as "Romanland."

For my part, it was when I began to focus on Roman identity that I realized how problematic the Byzantine rubric was. It turned out to be not a neutral label, under which we could safely correct the prejudices and distortions of the past, but indissolubly linked to those prejudices and acting as their main carrier. In much of the scholarship, it constituted an obstacle that prevented us from seeing realities that are otherwise clearly present in the sources. It blurred the differences between Romans and non-Romans and gave rise to an ideological paradigm that actively denied the Roman identity of our subjects, seeking various inventions, subterfuges, and rhetorical tricks to pretend that they were not who they claimed they were. These bad habits were forms of self-deception that, in many cases, created and perpetuated fictions. It also erected barriers of communication between our field and (ancient) Roman Studies. While our field was highly invested in tracing the lines of continuity between Byzantine society and the "Hellenistic" world (on the one hand) and early Christianity (on the other), it actively cut off lines of research that would lead back to ancient Rome. It seemed as if many scholars could not see past the label to the underlying realities, and those labels spun out realities of their own. The danger that mere names can weave fictional worlds around themselves, even in scholarship, will be taken seriously here. "Byzantium" insinuates an exotic world of mysticism, decadent luxury, aberrant sexuality, theocracy, absolutism, convoluted intrigue, and other aspects of sinister orientalism.

In the past few years, my thinking has made another quantum leap, as I am writing a book on western European perceptions of the eastern empire from late antiquity to World War II. Its tentative title is *Byzantium: Europe's Dark Mirror*. The insights gleaned from writing that book inform the arguments made below (full citations to sources and studies will be found there too). That book argues that western Europeans periodically reinvented the image of the eastern empire in ways that facilitated the emergence of a "western" and then "European" identity. That identity rested on cultural components that were appropriated to a significant degree from the eastern empire, including imperial Roman culture; the institutions, doctrines, and practices of imperial Christianity; and classical Greek literature and thought. These were recast as "belonging" to the west, and the east was imagined as their negative version, as their dark mirror, unworthy to claim them any longer after their initial invention. This process took various twists and turns over the centuries, so that what later came to be called "Byzantium" was already enmeshed in many overlapping layers of prejudice. It is pointless for the field to try to push back against them while keeping in place the name that has for so long acted as their linchpin. It is time to make a new start.

"Byzantium" interferes with our thinking when we try to understand the society that we are studying and makes it difficult to communicate our findings without resorting to distorting fictions. This term, along with its western medieval predecessor—the "empire of the Greeks"—was devised by people and institutions who were ideologically motivated to deny the identity of our subjects. It carries derogatory connotations, making our field into a subspecies of orientalism that promotes Eurocentric and colonial narratives at the expense of the people whom we study. It artificially severs east Roman society from its ancient roots and then segregates it historically, excluding it from broader discussions in which it could otherwise claim a leading role. Byzantium thereby becomes an artificial pocket-universe; it is "fictionalized as an extra-historical entity."[1]

In order to integrate it back into history, I have so far worked to restore the Byzantines' Roman identity from the primary sources, to change our perceptions by working from the ground up. It is now time to change the words that form the higher-order framework in which we work. If we are to abandon the Byzantine paradigm, we need an alternative with which to replace it. This alternative needs to reflect the self-perception of the people whom we study and their state, but it must also enable our field to take its place among the constellation of other neighboring fields without causing undue confusion. The present book, therefore, discusses the pros and cons of various alternatives that are being proposed or just being used provisionally until our field can have a focused discussion of the issue. Books and articles are being published that do not use "Byzantium" or "Byzantine" in their titles, when once that would have been de rigueur or at least unproblematic. They deal with a wide variety of topics, including history, religion, and identities, and refer instead to "east Rome," "east Romans," "the medieval Roman empire," or "the medieval east Roman world." The goal of the present book is to jump-start a more systematic discussion about how the field should reinvent itself.

In addition to east and medieval Romans (and medieval east Romans), I have also heard colleagues refer to Romeans, New Romans, and Orthodox east Romans. No one has yet made a clear and systematic case in favor of any of these alternatives, nor is it clear what field-name would result if it were adopted. They seem to be provisional and handy substitutes for the disfavored Byzantine label. There is a danger

---

I B. Anderson and M. Ivanova, "Introduction," in *Is Byzantine Studies a Colonialist Discipline?*, ed. Anderson and Ivanova, 10. Where a short-form citation is provided, please consult the Further Reading at the end.

here for a chaotic free-for-all that will land us in a position that has not been properly thought through, with less than ideal implications. We don't want to peer-pressure ourselves into a particular stance, and then work out the inevitable problems later. Too much rides on this, and we need to be intentional.

Therefore, I put other projects on hold in order to think through the issues at stake and present what I take to be a viable proposal to the field, which can, at a minimum, serve as a launching point for further discussion. On a practical level, until such a time as we are all on the same page the name of the field remains "Byzantine Studies," as reflected in the titles of our journals, book series, research institutes, and online presence. This is also how we and the history that we study are known to the public at large and to scholars in adjacent fields—that is, until we educate them otherwise. Our collective field identity, after all, like any identity, is not something that we can effectively change in a unilateral way. It requires buy-in from our peers as well as by popular media. My position at present, then, is one of having one foot in each world. I was trained as a Byzantinist and still refer to my field that way. But I now limit the Byzantine label to the subtitles of my books, to identify its research field in the broadest sense. Those who look more closely will find that inside my studies there are no "Byzantines" or "Byzantium," for these did not exist as historical entities, in the way in which those terms are understood.

In order to move forward, we must first articulate both the reasons for the change and a rationale for any specific new model that we adopt. The present book aims primarily to look to the future, and not get mired in a critique of the existing model. But it needs to explain what the main problems of that model are. These are quickly presented in the first chapter, for the benefit of readers who want to catch up to speed. The focus after that will be on weighing the options that stand before us for moving the field forward, including the pros and cons of different labels and their implications not only for history but also art history, the study of Orthodoxy, and the study of literature. In part, those fields need to be discussed apart from general history because they have different configurations and points of emphasis. Overall, this book attempts to think through the major issues involved in changing a field-name, not only on a general level but also at the level of practice in our various subfields as well.

I am optimistic that it will not be difficult to persuade our colleagues in other fields of our new identity. The case against the Byzantine rubric, and in favor of some kind of Roman one, is so obvious that it can be resisted only through a stubborn appeal to tradition. It should go without saying that tradition is a bad argument; indeed, it is not an argument at all. Interestingly, it is those who have been trained in Byzantine Studies and have learned all the subtle ways of evading or denying the truth that is plainly and transparently proclaimed in our sources who might be most inclined to resist change. I expect much less pushback from colleagues in adjacent fields, some of whom have been wondering why Byzantinists are still carrying on with all this denialism and cognitive dissonance, so long after they realized what nonsense it all is. I quote, for example, a leading historian of the caliphate, in the introduction to his recent translation of al-Baladhuri, a historian of the Arab conquests.

> The people of the so-called "Byzantine Empire" are variously referred to as Greeks in the Hitti translation [of al-Baladhuri] and as Byzantines in most of the modern secondary literature. I have chosen to call them Romans. This has the advantage that it reflects the word Rhomaioi, which they used to describe themselves, and Rūm, the Arabic word. Nobody at the time ever referred to them as "Byzantines" and nor will I.[2]

There are signs that historians of ancient Rome will also be receptive if we come out as east Roman historians.

2 H. Kennedy, *History of the Arab Invasions: The Conquest of the Lands. A New Translation of al-Balādhurī's Futūh al-Buldān* (London: Tauris, 2022) 16.

Ancient Roman identity is itself being seen in new ways, as more adaptable and diverse, so that an east Roman, Orthodox world is not beyond the imagination of ancient historians. Some are frankly admitting that "Byzantium" was unquestionably a phase of Roman history, even perhaps a Roman nation of sorts,[3] and, if they lack the expertise to extend their narratives into it, that can be done through a tighter collaboration between ancient and east Roman historiography. If the sheer duration of this state defeats the limits of our scholarly expertise, this is not a reason to deny that history happened as it did but rather to collaborate. If our narrow conceptions of scholarly expertise cannot cope with the timescales of the Roman polity, we should admit that frankly rather than deny its continuity simply in order to give comfort to our limitations.

There is also a generational shift taking place within Byzantine Studies. Few positions in the field were opened during the job crisis of the 1970s, which means that today there are few Byzantinists between the ages of 55 and 75. Yet the older generation is now almost completely retired, inactive, or deceased, which means that the field has come into the hands of scholars who are 55 or younger. But there is now another job crisis, and Byzantinists as such are not in demand. Departments of history are becoming increasingly and narrowly focused on modern history and expect new hires in "premodernity" to cover a lot of ground. It might be said that "Byzantium" already has name-recognition and that a new name will put us at a disadvantage. But that is not the case, if we respect the historical reality here. As it happens, no field could cover more ground than a "long Roman" one, spanning as it does from antiquity to the fifteenth century and beyond. It also features the most canonical empire in

---

3 E.g., W. V. Harris, *Roman Power: A Thousand Years of Empire* (Cambridge: Cambridge University Press, 2016) 113, 213–15, 239, 265, 314, and esp. 300. For diverse ancient Roman identities, see E. Dench, *Romulus' Asylum: Roman Identities from the Age of Alexander to the Age of Hadrian* (Oxford: Oxford University Press, 2005).

world history, with established recognition among historians of all periods. If the name-change proposed here is successful, new students of east Rome will be able to take both rhetorical and research advantage of this broader perspective. Without obliterating real historical differences that need to be reflected in our research, they would adapt to a job-market environment that increasingly lumps us all into one "premodern" basket. A Roman-centered pitch could work regardless of whether one studies the Julio-Claudians or the Komnenoi, Sallust or Psellos.

Acknowledgments

This book has benefited from discussions and debates with many colleagues, too many to list here. I want to thank especially those who read and commented on initial versions of the argument, including Stephanos Efthymiades, Garth Fowden, Dimitris Krallis, Marion Kruse, and Charis Messis. Anna Henderson at Arc Humanities Press read several versions of the book and offered excellent advice about how to improve the argument at all stages. I am also grateful to the readers for the press, who also caught a number of errors. A special thanks goes to Leonora Neville for many stimulating conversations about this topic, one of which was recorded for the podcast "Byzantium & Friends." Leonora will hopefully soon be publishing her own thoughts about this ongoing reinvention of our field.

Chapter 1

RIP Byzantium

The idea that the terms "Byzantium" and "the Byzantines" are traditional, and therefore hallowed by hoary heritage, is incorrect. These terms have been used in this way only since the later nineteenth century. They are barely 140 years old. There are turtles alive today that are older. But the field tells itself a different story. It is common to read that these terms were invented by the German philologist Hieronymus Wolf in the sixteenth century. This would make him, in a manner of speaking, the Father of Byzantine Studies, and he is often called that, in a way that is only half-ironic.

This origin story is wrong in every significant way. A close look at the evidence suggests that Wolf was not responsible for the use of "Byzantine" in the title of one of his editions. More importantly, it did not inaugurate a new paradigm for thinking about the eastern empire. Since around 800 AD, western Europeans had called it "the empire of the Greeks" and its subjects "the Greeks," and so did Wolf, his contemporaries, and his successors. This did not change in the sixteenth century, or even in the seventeenth and eighteenth. Edward Gibbon, for example, writing in the later eighteenth century, also called it "the Greek empire" and its subjects "the Greeks." He uses the terms "Byzantium" and "Byzantine" only as synonyms for "Constantinople" and "of Constantinople," just as those words had been used by the east Romans themselves, referring to the city only, not the empire as a whole and its entire population.

It was only after the Crimean War (1853–1856) that western scholarship moved away from the "Greek" paradigm and turned to a "Byzantine" one. It did so because of Great Power politics. Specifically, after 1821 there was a Greek state that aspired to expand at the expense of the Ottoman empire. In the west, Greece was often seen as aligned with Russia, which was almost never the case but it was at one important moment: the Crimean War. Greeks then joined Russia, which was fighting against Britain and France, and Greek fighters and newspapers hyped the slogan "Greek empire or death!" The Greek empire that they wished to revive was the very one that countless western textbooks discussed under that name. Not long afterward, historians writing in the western empires, which opposed this ambition to revive the Greek empire, retired that concept, as it implicitly legitimated Greek imperial irredentism. They replaced it with that of Byzantium or the Byzantine empire, which was non-committal when it came to the Greek question.

This summary inevitably simplifies a more complex process that had other causes too. But this was the context of the switch from the Greek to the Byzantine paradigm. In sum, the "Byzantine" rubric is not old. It comes from an era when Aryan race theory, craniometry, orientalism, and homeopathy were also trending. That era also witnessed the peak of European colonialism, a related phenomenon. To be sure, it was also when the foundations of many modern sciences were being laid and tremendous advances were made in understanding psychology, evolution, and the invisible economic engines of history. Unfortunately, the consolidation that took place then of "Byzantine Studies" as an academic field reflected more of the Eurocentric and orientalist side of nineteenth-century intellectual culture, and less its forward-looking breakthroughs. It codified and reaffirmed old prejudices while making no significant new discoveries, even though they were readily available to be plucked like low-hanging fruit. One had only to take seriously what our east Roman sources were telling us all along. Even when the Greek rubric was dropped in the later nineteenth century, what European scholars did *not* do was replace it with a more accurate Roman one, though some did urge exactly that at the time, most famously the Irish historian John B. Bury.[1]

The Byzantine paradigm for scholarship did not emerge from a study of the primary sources. It is not based on evidence and arguments but rather reflects political, ideological, and even geopolitical priorities. The same was true of the Greek paradigm that it replaced. The reason why western Europeans had called the east Romans "Greeks" for a thousand years before "Byzantium" kicked in was not because they had attained some insight into the truth of east Roman culture. At least, no such insight is ever communicated in western medieval and early modern writings. They called them Greeks specifically because it was the most convenient way by which they could deny their Romanness, a tradition and identity that two western institutions, namely the Church of Rome and the German empire, claimed for themselves. The existence of a Roman empire, a Roman emperor, and a Roman people in the east was an ideological inconvenience that western Europe brushed under the carpet of a disparaging Greek label. In other words, both of these labels—"empire of the Greeks" and "Byzantium"—exist in order to deny the identity of the east Romans and prevent it from interfering with western projects.

In other words, this was never only about names. It was primarily about "essences." Specifically, the essence of the eastern empire had to be "othered" from the perspective of the western European tradition. Now one might argue that it is still possible for historians to uncover the truth about a civilization even while giving it a false name. But this has not proven to be the case in our field. Modern scholarship in the twentieth century largely complied with the intended ideological purpose of this term and willfully blinded itself to many truths about the eastern empire. A great deal of nonsense

1 J. B. Bury, *A History of the Later Roman Empire from Arcadius to Irene (395 A.D. to 800 A.D.)*, 2 vols. (New York: Macmillan, 1889), 1:v–viii.

was published about the "essence" of Byzantine civilization. The point of these exercises was to show how different it was from the allegedly more authentic Roman tradition to which western Europe lay exclusive claim. In large part, our field was tricked into doing this by the name, or it hid behind the name while unnecessarily inventing essences. After all, scholars are people too, and they tend to assume that where there is a different name there must be a different essence. Even using a name for the purposes of periodization, in explicit awareness that this is a relatively arbitrary convention, can still lead historians to exaggerate differences between periods, perhaps in an effort to retroactively justify a period-break that, in turn, shaped how they were trained in grad school. Other scholars wrestle with the question of what exactly is "Byzantine" in Byzantine art or literature, forgetting that the term is a modern convention (if not an invention). Names matter, therefore, and this field in particular has proven itself unable to think past them.

At this point, it is useful to lay out in summary form the main reasons why the Byzantine rubric is problematic at present. At the time when it embarked upon its own, hopefully brief history, the Byzantine paradigm inherited many of the prejudices that were formerly attached to its "Greek" predecessor, though not all of them survive today and so do not need to be rehearsed here. For example, for many centuries—from the eighth to the fifteenth—one of the main charges leveled against "the Greeks" was that they were "disobedient" to the pope, i.e., they did not recognize papal supremacy and so were schismatic or heretical. This of course also contributed to the western medieval idea that they were not really Romans as they claimed and it aroused a great deal of hatred against the eastern Romans during the crusades. This prejudice was a powerful force behind the Fourth Crusade, which in 1204 conquered the city of Constantinople, destroyed much of it, and then dismembered the empire so that it could be ruled by western dukes and barons. The purpose of this violence was ostensibly to bring the Greeks "back" into obedience to the Mother Church of Rome, though in reality it promoted the interests of a few of the crusade's leaders. But this kind of religious polemic had waned by the time that Byzantium came to be studied academically in the west, many centuries later. The Reformation and wars of religion in Europe made the deviance of the Orthodox schismatics seem small by comparison. But for many centuries it had been a powerful matrix of bias against "the Greeks."

Therefore, the following discussion will leave aside specifically medieval polemics and focus on distortions that are still causing problems today. It is not comprehensive and will focus instead on the main ones.

The foremost problem is that "Byzantines" is not what our subjects called themselves, nor did they call their state "Byzantium." Now, in some cases scholars have to invent a name by which to refer to an ancient people whose own name is unknown. This is why we have "Minoans" on Bronze Age Crete, named after Minos, a Cretan king in Greek mythology (though the Minoans were not Greek). But we are not in such a situation. We are not in doubt as to what our subjects called themselves, for the evidence is overwhelming and speaks consistently on this point. They called themselves Romans, not (as so much modern scholarship claims) because they were confused, deluded, or putting on airs, but because they really were Romans by the same standards that Romans at any time in history have been Romans.

Accordingly, they also called their state the polity of the Romans. The name for it "on the street," in vernacular speech, was *Romanía*, i.e., "Romanland." (Note that the accent is on the *i*, as written here, not the *a*. By stressing it correctly, we can avoid confusing it with the modern country.) That name was established in popular speech by the fourth century, and by the tenth or eleventh it was being used as the state's formal name by its political authorities. Semantically, Romanía operates in the same way that "France" or "Germany" does today, i.e., it refers to a state that is named after the majority ethnic or national population in it. Seeing, then, as we have the authentic names of the people we study, we should use them and not impose other, made-up terms on them.

A second problem with the modern term "the Byzantines" is that it is not meant as a neutral "translation" of what our subjects meant by "the Romans." For example, the words "German" and "Greek" are understood today to be nothing more or less than the English equivalents of the German self-identifier *Deutsch* and the Greek self-identifier *Ellines*. But Byzantine Studies makes it emphatically clear that this is not how "the Byzantines" functions. It is a term that is introduced to deny that our subjects were who they said. In the usual formulation, repeated in countless publications, we are told that "the Byzantines may have called themselves Romans, *but* in reality they were not, because [insert invented reason that is arbitrarily favored by scholar x]." "The Byzantines" and "Byzantium" create a framework that denies our subjects' identity, as well as that of their state, so they cannot be treated as neutral "translations" of it. The field has never even pretended that it was doing that.

Incidentally, it should go without saying that denying a people's identity, especially when that was consistently and strongly held across fifteen centuries at all levels of their society, is, from a basic ethical standpoint, indefensible. Moreover, it is utterly unacceptable from a scholarly standpoint, which should, in such matters, rise to a higher level than just basic ethics. Scholars are supposed to understand and represent, and not become activists by denying historical claims of identity. Denial persists because Byzantine Studies was, from the start, embedded within the same Eurocentric and imperialistic ideologies that gave rise to it in the first place and have sustained it from medieval times to the present. But scholars writing in this vein are not trying to understand, they are trying to impose an outside ideology on our subjects and "keep them in their place" in the western order of things. Thus, the label Byzantium is caught up with frankly illegitimate practices of scholarship, and always has been.

The third problem is that we know exactly why and how this denial began, and whose interests it has served over the centuries. It has nothing to do with any kind of scholarly insight or research. The beneficiaries have changed over time, of course, but they are all broadly situated within the ambition of various western European powers and institutions to claim possession of the Roman legacy in order to assert some form of hegemonic dominion over their neighbors or the rest of the world, usually political and religious. These western European powers repeatedly appropriated cultural signifiers from the eastern empire in order to bolster their own credentials, while simultaneously denigrating the east Romans as mere Greeks and stripping them of the right to speak with Roman authority. The goods that the west appropriated in this way included all the modes and orders of the Roman imperial tradition, including court culture, titles, accessories, and laws; the Greek Patristic tradition of theology and Church Councils; and, starting in the fifteenth century, the tradition of Greek classical scholarship. In each case, the west took what it needed while denying that "the Greeks" had a right to it or asserting that they had forfeited that right. The denial of their Romanness was only a part of this broader appropriation.

Thus, we know exactly who created the edifice of denial and why. It is not a random mistake or fluke. It is not some hoary "tradition" that may be harmlessly indulged. It is a function of Eurocentrism and Euro-supremacy. "Byzantium" is only the current vehicle for it, after "empire of the Greeks" became problematic in the nineteenth century.

Denialism is also linked to western European colonialism in the Aegean. After all, this polemical approach to the east Romans facilitated their conquest by the Fourth Crusade and their exploitation by a range of western powers thereafter. Scholarship has followed in the footsteps of that act of conquest. I will give a tiny example. Modern scholars refuse to label the east Roman polity by its own name, Romanía, even though they know it (because it is recorded in many sources). But they *do* use that word when the crusaders arrive and begin to use it in their own narratives for the lands that they conquered, picking it up from the natives whom they subjected. So when east Roman sources say "Romanía," Byzantinists will write "Byzantium." But when French, Italian, or Latin sources after 1204 use the same word, Byzantinists will use it, so long as it refers to lands conquered by the westerners. Western usage is indulged, while east Roman usage is safely hidden away behind a "Byzantine" mask.

A fourth problem is the ontological temptation posed by names. This is the cognitive defect in human reasoning that leads us to think that, if something has a different name, it must also have a different "essence." An ontological division is thereby created, and scholarship devotes itself to the task of mapping out—that is, inventing—the traits of this allegedly different entity. This lends itself not only to scholarly confusion, but ideological mischief. Consider, for example, the argument by a Romanian national historian that seeks to appropriate "the Roman idea" for modern Romanian history as opposed to "the Byzantine idea," which, he argued, was "certainly an important element in the Romanians' identity, but a secondary and accidental one."[2] In such formulations, which are common even in mainstream Byzantine scholarship, the "essences" in question are so stratospherically lofty and abstract that it is hard to know what they even mean. In reality, they are reverse engineered to support an a priori conclusion, in this case about a modern national identity.

The Byzantine rubric suggests that some kind of qualitative rupture took place in Roman history, causing historians to exaggerate the significance of certain changes, such as Christianization, the Arab conquests, the presence of eunuchs at the court, or whatever else strikes their fancy, in order to retroactively justify the sense of rupture implied by the new name. In reality, there was no rupture between Roman and Byzantine history, no different "ideas" or "essences" at work. We are dealing instead with a long history of slow and gradual change. Greek, Roman, and Christian traditions were all in continual evolution over the course of centuries.

----

2 Nicolae Şerban Tanaşoca (1941–2017), critically discussed in D. Mishkova, *Rival Byzantiums: Empire and Identity in Southeastern Europe* (Cambridge: Cambridge University Press, 2023), 283.

Each changed gradually as it adapted to each other. What, in this mix, might have caused a significant rupture? Was it Christianity? This would imply that Romans could not be Christians. But that not only sounds wrong (because it is), but incidentally refutes the entire field of "late antiquity," which is premised on the Christianization of Roman society. Was it perhaps the "demography" (to put it euphemistically) of the eastern empire? But I have yet to see an argument that Romans could not come from the east (in fact, the ancient Roman origin myth goes back to Trojan settlers who moved west). At any rate, it is naïve to expect rigorous argumentation here, or any argumentation. That is not how this sad exercise is usually done. The Byzantine "essence" was not discovered and elaborated through research: it was instead reverse engineered from the need to endow the name with content, and the name was invented and then imposed for political and ideological reasons.

What was the "essence" of Byzantium? In practice, the Byzantine rubric came prepackaged with content that it inherited from its "Greek" predecessor, meaning the perception of the "empire of the Greeks" by western Europeans. That is why the term Byzantine encapsulates a bundle of mostly negative associations. These had been attributed to the easterners by Europeans in the Middle Ages and early modernity; they included treachery, duplicity, intrigue, excessive rhetorical subtlety, religious deviance, lack of manliness (e.g., on the battlefield), effeminacy (too many women and eunuchs in power), decadent luxury, and exoticism. In the medieval period, the religious deviance in question was the refusal to bow before the Church of Rome, whereas in the Enlightenment it took the form of irrational mysticism, superstition, theocracy, and an excess of pious zeal, to which were added cruelty, disloyalty, and a lack of civic virtue. In short, this was a species of orientalism. Orientalism refers to western representations of the east that render it ideologically inferior to the west and needing western discipline and subjugation in order to function properly.[3] This is precisely how the ideological apparatus of western prejudice against "the Greeks" worked in occupied Romanía after 1204. This was a project of colonial rule that was both fueled in advance and justified in retrospect by an orientalist view of "the Greeks."

Byzantine scholarship has been laboring for decades to push back against these specific prejudices, but each scholar takes on only a part of the picture. In aggregate, however, this amounts to pushing back against the Byzantine paradigm as a whole. That is what this book is attempting to do, for when all is said and done there is no sanitized version of "Byzantium" left after it has been fully purged of these prejudices and false associations. All it ever consisted of was that. And even if we refute all that nonsense, the Byzantine label will always act as a back door through which they will sneak back in. Consider the eleventh-century figure Michael Psellos. Calling him "a Byzantine courtier" is an entirely different thing than calling him "an east Roman polymath and politician." The former label was used to depict him as a sinister, duplicitous, and Machiavellian character, who helped to destroy the empire in the eleventh century. This image was ubiquitous down to the end of the twentieth century. But the latter label does not do that kind of work, nor does it conjure an equivalent personality-type.

Leonora Neville has made this argument about Anna Komnene, daughter of the emperor Alexios I Komnenos (1081–1118) and one of the first women to write a fully-fledged history. Calling her "a Byzantine princess" means something quite different from, and worse than, calling her "a Roman historian."[4] Now, one might respond that these are not equiv-

---

3 An idea, set forth by E. Said, *Orientalism* (New York: Pantheon, 1978), in a problematic way but at its core an undeniable thesis.

4 See episode 43 of the podcast Byzantium & Friends, entitled "Is it time to abandon the rubric 'Byzantium'?, with Leonora Neville," posted on February 11, 2021, available at https://byzantiumandfriends.podbean.com/e/43-is-it-time-to-abandon-the-rubric-byzantium-with-leonora-neville/.

alent terms to begin with, and that we should be comparing the valence of "Byzantine princess" to that of "Roman princess" (on the one hand) or "Byzantine historian" to "Roman historian" (on the other). But that is to miss the ideological tendencies of the two paradigms. The Byzantine one ensures that Anna, even though she was a historian, will also or even primarily be called a "Byzantine princess," with all the sinister traits that implies. Conversely, there is no such thing as "Roman princess" in our vocabulary; the term is almost meaningless. Byzantium had princesses, who meddled in politics and dominated their men. That was how our field long saw Anna, not as a "Roman historian." The two paradigms are not equivalent to begin with, for they push our subjects into different frames of reference. The names create the essences, as the tail wags the dog.

A fifth problem is that "Byzantine," by postulating a different essence, severs the eastern empire from its ancient roots and thereby makes it harder for scholars to bridge the divide in order to study connections and long-term trends. This severance has worked in specific ideological ways. In the Enlightenment model of the eastern empire, the latter was made up of the "bad" versions of the constitutive elements of European civilization, namely ancient Greece, Rome, and Christianity. Europe aspired to own or emulate the good versions of those three, and cast the eastern empire as the embodiment of all their degenerate versions. Politically it was despotic, tyrannical, and lacking in civic virtue. Linguistically, it spoke and wrote a degenerate version of Greek. The spoken language was corrupt and the written one produced nothing but rhetorical obfuscation. Religiously too, its Orthodox faith was supposed to represent everything that the Enlightenment thinkers disliked about Christianity: it was irrational, superstitious, theocratic, and intolerant. This was the tripartite formula from which the model of "Byzantium" was constructed. All the right elements were there—of course they were, because western Europe took most of them from the east!—but they were present in the "wrong" way.

Much of this has been toned down or quietly retired today, especially on the religious side. But the underlying prejudices are alive among classicists and ancient historians, often blocking them from looking too "late" lest they be associated with the prejudices that attach to that material. They have erected disciplinary boundaries between fields, with classical Greek studies almost defining itself in opposition to texts that are too "late," Christian, or "Byzantine." Calling a text Byzantine is enough to caution most classicists away from it. Even when they have to work with Byzantine materials—including the manuscripts of the ancient authors, scholia, and commentaries!—they fiercely and defensively resist the notion that this makes them "Byzantinists." They have internalized the mentality that classical and Byzantine are polar opposites, and they need to maintain professional purity, lest their colleagues think that they have strayed into questionable terrain and lost their classicist identities. There are jobs and careers at stake in all this, it is not a trivial matter.

I have the strong suspicion that if our texts were called "east Roman" they would not elicit such allergic reactions. This suspicion is confirmed by the general success of the relatively recent field of "late antiquity." Many of its core texts used to be seen as "early Byzantine," but the rebranding made them acceptable to many Classics programs. The same goes for Roman history. Histories of ancient Rome lamely peter out at whatever random point each scholar arbitrarily decides that "this isn't Rome anymore." The cut-off is justified with vague gestures toward despotism, eunuchs, Christianity, too much Greek, or just whatever. A few have the honesty to admit that this is arbitrary and that they have told only part of the Roman story. But if ancient Rome were followed by "east Rome" rather than "Byzantium," a lot of this nonsense might evaporate, allowing a more productive relationship to emerge between the two fields.

This works in the other direction too, in the engagement by Byzantinists with the ancient world, but only with respect to the Roman tradition. Scholars of Byzantine literature are usually trained in the classics, and scholars of Byzantine

Orthodoxy are likewise usually trained in early Christianity. But when it comes to the ancient Roman tradition, there is a pronounced divide, which in reality is an artificial trench. It is widely assumed among Byzantinists that Byzantium had little to do with ancient Rome and that there is little to learn from looking too closely at it, as if a reset had occurred at some (unspecified) point that wiped the political slate clean. This is partly why Byzantinists treat the Bishop Eusebios of Kaisareia's theological-political orations in praise of Constantine the Great as quasi-constitutional founding texts of the new order, and almost never look to earlier periods of Roman history to find relevant background for Byzantine thought and practice. This approach is wrong on many levels, and it also leaves much potentially exciting research on the table. It too stems from the field's original sin, Roman denialism. Ancient Roman material is off the table, though the same is not the case for classical Greek or early Christian material.

A sixth problem is that the prejudices associated with the Byzantine brand have seeped into the public consciousness, from where they may prove difficult or impossible to remove. Every few days I come across a reference in journalism, or even in academic writing in another field, to the "Byzantine" nature of a highly complex social, economic, or political system, a way of saying that it is unnecessarily convoluted and tangled and designed to exclude and confuse outsiders. It is not a flattering term, and often implies malice (e.g., subscription services are making it harder for customers to cancel "by knowingly complicating the process through byzantine procedures").

The use of this term seems to be growing more common as our economies and social-media experiences become more complicated. While this specific usage is first attested in the 1930s, it emerged from the same core set of prejudices about Byzantium that were current in the nineteenth century. "Byzantium" was never a neutral term, not in any European language of that era. In Italy, for example, it referred to the dysfunctions of the nascent Italian state, especially in the south. In Prussia, it was used to characterize court intrigue.

These prejudices were current at precisely the time when the "founders of the field" settled on the term Byzantine Studies, for example Karl Krumbacher, who founded the first journal in the field in 1892, *Byzantinische Zeitschrift*. Men in his position were aware of the prejudices associated with the name, but did nothing to combat them, because they by and large embraced them.

Computer scientists still use the term "Byzantine" to refer to malicious and duplicitous programs that are designed in bad faith, and sometimes as a synonym for "irrational" and "terrorist." Some of them bristle when it is pointed out that this usage is unnecessarily offensive. "There are no Byzantines around now, so who cares?", is a standard response. (Note that these words come from university professors.) The Association of Computing Machinery was advised by one of its members to recommend against this use of the word, in the context of its initiative "Words Matter." Initially the Association refused, but determined remonstrations brought it around to adding "Byzantine" to a list of discouraged words (along with "master / slave" and the like).[5] Yet many in that field still use it. "Tradition," you see.

The Byzantine name offers few, if any, advantages. Some may be attracted to a field that is perceived as exotic, esoteric, and incomprehensible to outsiders. One day on a street in Syracuse, Sicily, I was even told that my field sounds exotic, fun, and appealing because its name has a *y* in it and *z*, which give it the seductive charm, almost like a fantasy world. Why change it?, I was asked. But if these, along with "tradition," are the name's saving graces, it is not long for this world.

A seventh problem is that "Byzantium" suggests affinities with the Slavic Orthodox world, and specifically with Russia, meaning both the tsarist empire and the Soviet Union. In western eyes since the early nineteenth century, this perceived affinity has served to alienate the eastern empire from the west, situating it even further away from the

---

5 See www.acm.org/diversity-inclusion/words-matter

ancient Roman tradition. There are countless books and articles that posit the allegedly sick and twisted political world of Byzantium as the matrix of all the pathologies that are supposed to characterize Russia, from its authoritarianism and theocracy to back-stabbing intrigue and dissimulation. In his famous book *The Clash of Civilizations*, Cold War theorist Samuel Huntington built on this connection to postulate an "Orthodox" cultural block that originated in Byzantium and encompassed modern Russia.[6] He did so with little analysis or critical scrutiny of the relevant civilizations: the "Byzantium" that he encountered in the secondary literature pointed him obviously in that direction. Had he instead encountered an "east Rome" with deep roots in antiquity, the case would not have been so obvious. He would have had to argue for it.

The same affinity has also been depicted positively, most prominently in Dimitri Obolensky's *Byzantine Commonwealth*, which influenced Huntington. This posited a continuum of Orthodox cultures spanning from Byzantium to its Slavic neighbors.[7] It is a framework that reflected Obolensky's own Slavic and Orthodox bias and was enabled by the specific notion of "Byzantium" that he was working with, whose cultural essence was Greek Orthodoxy. There is not a trace of Romanness in his understanding of the culture. His book, which became quite popular, cemented the "essence" of Byzantium as belonging to the eastern, Slavic, and Orthodox world, thereby confirming long-held western European biases.

---

6 S. Huntington, *The Clash of Civilization and the Remaking of World Order* (New York: Touchstone, 1997) esp. 50, 140–41, 160. See also A. Gurevitch, "Why am I not a Byzantinist?" *Dumbarton Oaks Papers* 46 (1992) 89–96; S. Takács, *The Construction of Authority in Ancient Rome and Byzantium: The Rhetoric of Empire* (Cambridge: Cambridge University Press, 2009).

7 D. Obolensky, *The Byzantine Commonwealth: Eastern Europe, 500–1453* (New York: Weidenfield & Nicholson, 1971). For more discussion the "Commonwealth," see Chapter 3 below, section on "Roman Orthodoxy".

There are strong reasons to be skeptical of models that link the eastern Roman empire in its essence or even its historical trajectory to Russia, both the negative and the positive models. It was the "Byzantine" rubric that enabled both to see the light of day. It is, in fact, possible to explain the ideological mechanisms through which this happened. The eastern empire had, in western perception, been stripped of its Romanness since medieval times. In the nineteenth century, it was further stripped of its long-standing (and essentially racial) identification with "the Greeks." That left Orthodoxy as its sole remaining cultural marker. This is why studies of Byzantium produced during the twentieth century are obsessed with Orthodoxy, trying to explain everything about the culture, even its most secular aspects, as derivations of some deep-seated Orthodox essence. This strengthened its identification with Russia and the broader (mostly Slavic) Orthodox world. Not only that, Byzantium's alleged absolutism enabled it to function as the matrix of the Soviet Union too. All these are fictions, of course, but fictions that are distorted into a plausible form by the funhouse mirrors of Byzantine Studies.

There are other points that I could mention, but the first one is decisive by itself. If we add the second and third, the tradition of Byzantine Studies begins to look like a caricature of an academic field. Nevertheless, a great deal of excellent research has taken place within it, despite the biased framework in which it has had to operate and which often works against it. It is time for the field to cast off that old and rotten shell and emerge with new colors. What shall those be?

Chapter 2

Contenders for a New Field-Name

Academic fields have emerged to study specific periods, regions, languages and literatures, states, cultures, religions, movements, wars, or methodologies regardless of where and when they are applied. In short, there are fields to study all the ways in which we chop up history. They are named after their primary subject matter, in a direct and concise way, for convenience and possibly in order to say something about the field's relationship to its peers.

Byzantine Studies has always been oriented around the Byzantine state, so-called Byzantium. Accordingly, "the Byzantines" have always been seen as the subjects of that state. This does not mean that all Byzantine research studies the state; far from it. But whether one works on texts, art, religion, archaeology, or whatever else, often without the state being directly relevant to the matter at hand, it is nevertheless generally called "Byzantine" only if it relates in some way to life in the Byzantine state or was adjacent to it (geographically or chronologically). By contrast, studies of ancient Greece or the medieval West are not oriented around a single state in the same way, but rather around clusters of polities that made up a vaguely coherent cultural block in the eyes of scholars and possibly even of the people who lived at the time. But histories of ancient Rome and of Byzantium have always been histories of the Roman state, its politics, wars, society, and culture. This was true of the histories written at the time, by both the ancient Romans and the "Byzantines" themselves, and it remains true of the histories written about them since. The Byzantines called their state "the polity of the Romans" or *Romanía*; medieval Europeans called it the empire of the Greeks; and modern scholars call it the Byzantine empire.

In the case of Byzantium, this state-oriented conception of the field holds together relatively well because the state in question happens to have been one of the most coherent, centrally consolidated, and effectively run state projects in all premodern history. For most of its history and over most of its territory at any time, there was only one legitimate political authority in Romanía that enforced a single legal framework, implemented a uniform system for assessing and collecting taxes, recruited a single army from the entire Roman territory, and recognized only one official religion, successfully persecuting most of its rivals out of existence. The social system was relatively uniform across the state territories. The dominant language was Greek, especially after the seventh century, and its art forms were fairly uniform too, again especially after the seventh century. The Roman state played a huge role in keeping all this together. This was true not only on a merely practical, infrastructural level, but also in terms of mentalities. The ideology of the eastern Roman state "offered the only framework through which people could understand their world and through which political, social, and other forms of social discourse could be comprehended."[1] The vast majority of the population self-identified as Roman in both an ethnic and a legal sense. No western European state exhibited this level of consolidation until early modern times.

If you were to step outside the borders of the east Roman state and travel into the Islamic world, into the Caucasus region, into the steppe north of the Black Sea, or into Bulgaria, Raška (Serbia), or central Italy, one would find oneself

---

1 J. Haldon, *The Empire that Would not Die: The Paradox of Eastern Roman Survival, 640–740* (Cambridge, MA: Harvard University Press, 2016), 191; see also 124.

in a significantly different world, where language, culture, customs, social structure, state apparatus, law, and likely religion would all be different. To put it in terms of scholarship, one would find oneself in a different academic field. It therefore makes sense to organize research around the Byzantine state, as scholarship has always done, whether the research itself is directly about the state or not.

This choice is analytically valid and does not by itself reflect a particular moral stance toward Byzantium. To mention a few extremes, there are people who dislike this state as the alleged matrix of Russian and Soviet absolutism, or as the killer of ancient Hellenic culture, while a few on the Orthodox fundamentalist side glorify it as the historical expression of Christian nationalist militarism. None of these groups produces first-rate scholarship or has much of an impact on the field. Professional scholars may question "the strength and beneficence of the Byzantine state, the pliancy of its subjects, its dazzling image in the eyes of its neighbors, and even its coherence as a stable object of analysis."[2] These are legitimate questions, though I am skeptical about the last one. If the Byzantine state is not a coherent or stable object of analysis, then nothing in history is. To destabilize it as an object, we have to enter a Heraclitean realm of infinite ontological fluidity. This would, then, have to extend to every state or social formation that has ever existed, and it must also question the coherence of our individual selves too, the narratives that, we believe, constitute us as singular persons. This is, in philosophy and in certain domains of physics, a legitimate enterprise, but it is not one on which historical research can be reliably grouped into fields. I am personally happy to have that discussion, but it points to a philosophical conception of reality whose implications are so profound that the issues raised in this book are trivial by comparison, if not irrelevant.

---

2 B. Anderson and M. Ivanova, "Introduction," in *Byzantine Studies*, ed. Anderson and Ivanova, 26–27.

Field-names have to be relatively concise. By necessity, they operate at a high level of abstraction and so inevitably cannot capture all the "nuance" that modern scholarship prizes. They are meant to encapsulate vast areas of research, including all the debates that take place under the rubric of the common name. Field-names do not necessarily reflect the identities and concerns of the people who are studied by them, nor are they always even recognizable by them. People in the Middle Ages, for example, had no awareness that they were living in the Middle Ages, and so that rubric has nothing to do with their self-conception. Ancient Spartans did not spend much of their time thinking about what it meant to be Greek (Hellenic), though that overarching identity was a meaningful part of their lives. Field-names, therefore, do not necessarily or always reflect the identity of their subjects, but it is preferable when they do and imperative that they do so in a non-derogatory way. "Byzantium" fails on that count. It not only offends, it is specifically meant to distort reality when non-distorted alternatives are available.

Field-names that offend are gradually being replaced. I mention here only the replacement of the term "Oriental" in Anglo-American academic institutions, including research institutes and learned associations. The Oriental Institute of the University of Chicago was recently renamed The Institute for the Study of Ancient Cultures. The American Society of Oriental Research recently renamed itself The American Society of Overseas Research, thereby preserving its acronym. You can read about the rationale behind these changes in the statements that were issued by these institutions. US President Barack Obama issued an executive order that the term "oriental" could no longer be used by federal agencies. It is not only academic institutions that are under pressure to remove offensive labels. Football teams with racist names are also facing such calls. Dixie State University (in Utah) is changing its name to Utah Tech University, as the term "Dixie" alludes to the pro-slavery Confederacy during the American Civil War.

More examples can be mentioned, but I will stop here because, in a certain sense, they are irrelevant to our task. Each field has a unique history and so the reasons for keeping or changing its name should be examined on their own terms in light of that name's history and ideological associations. Therefore, replacing the rubric Byzantium does not depend on the justice or logic of changes undertaken by other fields, institutions, or corporate enterprises. It rests on the problems with the name itself, as briefly itemized in the previous chapter, and on the emerging consensus in our field that it is time to move on and shake off this distorting label, a legacy of western Eurocentrism and ideological Euro-supremacy.

A key function performed by field-names is to facilitate coordination and liaise with adjacent areas of research, to distinguish one from the other and mark their territories and potential sites of overlap and collaboration. This is especially crucial in our case, for if we were to follow the indicators in our sources about the name that our field should have, it would simply be Roman Studies, for that was the name borne by the state in question and the majority of its subjects. Moreover, this phase of the Roman state and history of the Roman people lasted longer than its ancient counterpart, so on that criterion we have more of a claim to the label than historians of ancient Rome. But renaming Byzantine Studies simply as Roman Studies will not work in practice, because that domain-name is already "taken," in a sense, and it would create confusion. By not claiming that label in its unqualified form, we are already making a major concession to our colleagues on the ancient side. One day, it is possible that their field and ours will merge, as Bury envisaged 125 years ago. This may happen for happy reasons, such as the realization that we all work on the same story, or for unhappy reasons, such as the downsizing and consolidation of research fields in the humanities into fewer units. In all likelihood, if it happens, it will be for a combination of reasons. For now, our fields remain distinct, which is in many ways necessary, though they do not need to be so cut off from each other as they currently are. Hopefully this will change, especially if the present proposal is accepted. But at present, a merger would be too much, too soon. First we have to clean up the damage caused by the Byzantine rubric and advance a model that serves as an intermediary to a merger, or to stand on its own indefinitely if that's how it turns out.

These remarks reveal that field-names are also a function of its "diplomacy" with the public and other fields. But we are also in the fortunate position of choosing a name that validates the identity of our subjects as Romans and of their state as the polity of the Romans, as opposed to sticking with a name that was meant to deny them. In fact, *it is already possible to do this* on a substantive level even within the Byzantine rubric. I just published a long history of this society in which I never had to refer to them by any other name than their own or to qualify it (the exception being in southern Italy, where two different ideas of who was "Roman" were in play, and so disambiguation was in order). Even in a technical article on, say, tenth-century issues, so long as the study is identified as dealing with the eastern or Byzantine empire in its various metadata (such as in its title, subtitle, venue of publication, etc.), there is no reason to refer to the people in question or their state as anything other than Roman. The context and metadata of publication suffice to authorize an unqualified usage. In other words, in specialized research, where the *who* and *when* are already clear in advance, there is no reason to use the Byzantine label or even a qualified Roman one ("east Romans") within the pages of the study. Qualification is necessary only to distinguish our Romans from any others, and this is rarely necessary in most specialized research.

But at the level of the field-name, where that metadata operates, we have to learn now to tell a different story. Ideally, the field-name must respect the proper names of our subjects (on the one hand) and negotiate with adjacent fields (on the other hand). We therefore need a qualified Roman brand-name to replace Byzantium. The rest of this book will consider the pros, cons, and implications of the options that

I have heard from colleagues, including medieval Romans, new Romans, Romaeans, and east Romans.

I am confident that much will be gained by dropping the Byzantine rubric, which continues to marginalize and exoticize our field, exclude it from important discussions where it might otherwise play an important role, and make it unable to interface well with other fields. It makes it harder to see our subjects as real people. I am sometimes asked by colleagues in other fields why we continue using these terms when we ourselves know they are a fiction, one burdened by considerable prejudice at that. It is now fairly widely known, even among many non-specialists, that there was no such thing as "the Byzantines," so for our field to carry on with this nonsense is to risk contempt as well.

Conversely, we have little to lose. The only "credit" that Byzantium receives routinely in the west consists of two points, first that it "saved" Europe from Arab invasion from the east and, second, that it "preserved" classical literature so that western scholars could study them properly after the Renaissance. These points are Eurocentric insofar as they measure the value of a civilization in terms of what it did for western Europe. Beyond that, the brand-image of Byzantium among the general public is basically garbage. In media and journalism, the word refers to excessive complexity with a whiff of deception and double-dealing. Additionally, we have commodities that the brand-name is used to market. One cluster plays on "decadent luxury" or a particular aesthetic splendor in order to sell bath soaps, lotions, jewelry, runway couture, and the like. Another peddles mysticism to a mal-aised bourgeoisie who want to feel a frisson of spirituality and profundity. It draws on general associations of the east with mysticism and is used to sell icons, spiritual literature, museum tickets, and other paraphernalia. All this I would be happy to shoot into the sun. If our academic field moves on and these industries continue to use the label in this way, fine. Their brand category will increasingly become just a fantasy label used to sell products, detached from the civilization that we study, and will validate our decision to abandon it.

"Medieval Romans"?

One alternative to Byzantine that some are using is "medieval Roman." This recuperates Roman identity, while qualifying it as medieval, to distinguish our subjects chronologically from the ancient Romans. The eastern Roman polity lasted from the fourth to the fifteenth century, a period that is coterminous with the western Middle Ages, making for a good chronological fit. To be sure, there is some ambiguity about when the Middle Ages began, both in the west and the east, especially given the recent expansion of the competing period of "late antiquity," which has swallowed up everything between the third and the seventh centuries. Figures of the fourth century such as Julian, Gregory of Nazianzos, and Theodosius I are late ancient Romans and cannot convincingly be characterized as medieval Romans. Perhaps, then, we could stipulate that in the east the medieval period begins in the seventh century. Would it make sense to call our subjects "medieval Romans" after that? Obviously, as mentioned above, we would not have to call them that every time they were mentioned. In discussions that were primarily concerned with them and their world, they would simply be Romans, with the medieval qualification added only when it was necessary to distinguish them from their ancient predecessors.

However, a number of factors make the qualification "medieval" less than ideal for scholarly practice. To be sure, in some general contexts it may work fine, but in some decisive contexts the category "medieval" is just as problematic as the "Byzantine" one that it would be replacing. Before we discuss these problems, I want to emphasize that the following discussion pertains to the specific field-name with which we want to replace Byzantine Studies and its cognates (Byzantium and the Byzantines). It is not about whether this field, under whatever name, may then take its place among the broader constellation of fields that may collectively be grouped as medieval for purposes of coordination. That is a separate question to which I will return at the end.

I begin with a practical problem posed by a medieval field-name. "Medieval Romans" is ambiguous because it fails to distinguish the Romans of the east from those of the city of Rome, which remained a major population center and power in the medieval period. In the medieval west, "the Romans"— that is, the people of Rome—constituted a more or less discrete group with their own identity. Our new category would therefore be ambiguous from the get-go. A hypothetical *Journal of Medieval Roman Studies* would have a confusing title.

The same is true about the name "medieval Roman empire," which I have seen in print and heard at conferences as an alternative to "Byzantium." When the audience consists mostly of experts in this field, they know what is meant. But western medievalists will be confused, because for many centuries the medieval German Reich called itself "the Roman empire" too, and that was the mantle that it wore in the political hierarchy and ideological debates of medieval western Europe. Somewhat later it was known as the "Holy Roman Empire" (whose full title was filled out with the words "of the German nation"). Now, the Romanness of this German empire had little to do with the ancient Roman empire or Romanía in the east (the latter being an extension of the former). Moreover, it understood its Romanness in ways that would have been quite unfamiliar to most actual Romans, whether of antiquity or of the east, but there is no doubt that for a time its rulers believed themselves to be the emperors of the Romans and monarchs of the Roman empire. While a strong case can be made that the eastern Roman polity was far more Roman than its German counterpart, I would not want its new name to rest on the success of such an argument, nor to create unnecessary friction with our western medieval colleagues. We also do not need to create more confusion. As matters stand, when scholars of western Europe refer to "the medieval Roman empire," they mean the German one, not the one in the east. Internet search results tend to bear this out.

Beyond these confusions, the term "medieval" poses at least five major ideological problems, relating to what the term "medieval" signifies and how it would impact our field if we adopted it as part of its field-identity. The following, then, are arguments against its adoption.

The first is that "medieval" has negative connotations in popular parlance, as medievalists themselves often note and lament. To be sure, specialist research is not overly affected by this and, for the most part, medievalists carry on with their work as if the issue did not exist. They know that the label "medieval" is artificial and does not correspond to the identity of their subjects. Yet in the culture at large, the Middle Ages are habitually associated with barbarism, cruelty, superstition, theocracy, intolerance, and irrationality, and a great many misconceptions are foisted onto it, such as that medieval people believed that the earth was flat and regularly burned witches. These errors, although repeatedly refuted by experts, have proven to be tenacious and impossible to remove from public awareness. They continue to be repeated by politicians, celebrities, journalists, and even public educators.

This stereotyping of the Middle Ages is no accident, nor a trivial aspect of modern societies. It is, in fact, constitutive of the very project of modernity itself, which from the start imagined itself as a departure from the troubles that assailed western Europe in medieval times. When its emerging nations began to present themselves as enlightened, civilized, and embarking on a path of development, they did so by demonizing a host of Others, including the Orient and the "savages" of the New World and Africa. In fact, "Byzantium" acquired much of its negative reputation this way, for it too was cast as one of Europe's many repudiated and demonized Others. The medieval past of Europe itself was among the A-list of modernity's Others. "Medieval" stood for all the bad stuff that lay in Europe's past and that modernity aspired to overcome. The term began life in this way, even if at first only to refer to the barbarous Latin that was being written after the fall of the Roman empire and before the revival of proper Latinity by the humanists of the Renaissance. The concept of the "medieval" is thus inextricably bound to the ideological project of modernity and its polemics against non-European cultures and European premodernity itself. It seems unlikely that the term will shed this baggage soon. Therefore, our field, which is seeking to make a clean new start by shedding past stereotypes, would be ill-advised to take on the baggage of other fields. Moreover, Romanía did not share in signature traits of "medieval" societies: it did not launch crusades; it did not lose touch with the classical tradition, such that it later required a Renaissance to rediscover it; it did not witness divisive conflicts or wars between church and state; and it did not break down into feuding lordships. Just as we would be ill-advised to take on the public-relations problems of the medieval rubric, as historians we should not imply that our society shared in such traits with its western European counterparts.

The second ideological problem is that the term "medieval" reflects a periodization of history that is not applicable to New Rome and its civilization. The Middle Ages were invented in hindsight, to refer to a period of darkness and decline that allegedly befell western Europe after the end of Roman rule there, before the revivals heralded by the humanists of the Renaissance, especially the recovery of classical learning, and later by the Enlightenment. The Middle Ages referred to all that fell in between the classical (ancient) and the modern. But this trajectory, whose reality is dubious even for western Europe, is inapplicable to the east Roman polity, whose scholars never lost touch with classical Greek literature and whose state never broke down into petty feudal fragments.

The eastern Roman polity was a direct extension of its ancient predecessor, with no disruptions in its history and state infrastructure such as marked western Europe. There was no loss of statal continuity, community identities, or traditions of scholarship. None of this had to be reinvented or reconstituted on new grounds. There was always a *basileus* of the Romans (almost always in Constantinople); the Church and bureaucracy continued to operate and changes to them were gradual and incremental; the army units were directly descended from those of antiquity (sometimes even preserving the same names); and the language and traditions of higher education were marked by a great deal of continuity from the fourth to the fifteenth centuries. To be sure, east Rome and its culture had its ups and downs, but it would be inaccurate to apply the paradigm of a Middle Ages to its over-all trajectory. In addition, western Europe exited the Middle Ages at precisely the moment Romanía ceased to exist, so there was no modernity for the east Roman state. "Medieval" is a term that forces the mind to think along the lines of a fall and a Renaissance, followed by modernity. These contours do not fit the east. The arc of ancient—medieval—modern does not apply. If we pick up the medieval rubric, we will have to be explaining this over and over again at every turn, as many Byzantinists already have to do to explain to outsiders how Byzantium was *not* like western Europe in this regard. Adopting the "medieval" rubric would only exacerbate this problem. It would force us to keep explaining the differences of our field from the west.

The third problem with "medieval" is that it not only pos-its a specific configuration of time, a formless kind of "in-betweenness," but it also links identity to temporality: it pos-its that the identity of east Roman civilization was a function of *when* it existed, namely contemporaneously with the medi-eval west. In many respects, however, temporality tells us less about it than the ancient matrix from which it emerged. The fundamental modes and orders of Romanía—political, social, economic, literary, and religious—were laid down in the period between 150 and 450 AD. To understand how the culture of east Rome worked in, say, the tenth century, one has to be well versed in the major developments of that ear-lier period, and far less so in anything that was going on in the medieval west or in the Islamic east in the tenth century. The creation of Constantinople, the Councils of the Church, and the establishment of the gold currency explain more about later Roman history than do, say, the terrible state of the papacy in the tenth century or the rise of the Hamdanids at Aleppo. Genealogy in these cases is more important than mere contemporaneity. This, by the way, was uniquely true of

Romanía in this period, as it was the oldest state in the world and, by and large, it remained true to its ancient modes. Its relationship to an ancient formative period was more consequential for it than for any other contemporaneous society, whether western or Islamic.

Romanía was not, then, medieval in the same way that western Europe was. It was not entirely "of" its time. It was a far older culture, adapting to a changing world while preserving its ancient modes. Yet the "medieval" rubric severs those connections and defines the culture through mere contemporaneity. To be clear, I am not arguing that this view of Romanía, in which genealogy counts more than contemporaneity, should be encoded and prioritized in our new labels for the field. But neither should the opposite view, which is what "medieval" represents. We should adopt labels that are neutral as to this question, so that scholars can discuss it without the field-name putting its finger on the scales. "Medieval" would prioritize periodization and again postulate ruptures based on mere chronology. Given the ontological temptation discussed above, scholars would feel the need to explain when the eastern empire became properly medieval. This would just be another factory of fictions.

This brings me to the fourth problem, namely the specific institutions and developments that are evoked by the term "medieval," which had no counterparts in Romanía. Medievalists are understandably unhappy that their field-name points only to an otherwise formless "in-betweenness," and some have tried to define this period though more specific traits that impart a coherence of sorts to the diversity of cultures that existed in the medieval west. The most prominent of these include feudalism; the gradual separation of secular and spiritual authority and the tension that emerged between them; and the slow trajectory of state formation, starting from barbarian kingdoms run by warlords to feudal tessellation and finally to the rise of the proto-nation-states. However, none of these are remotely relevant to the experience of east Rome. Its social, legal, economic, and political institutions were never feudal, and the attempt to interpret them as such in order to integrate the study of "Byzantium" into that of medieval Europe has proven disastrous and has been rejected by almost all Byzantinists who have commented on the issue. If we go by the near-total absence of feudalism from current discussions, it would seem that the concept has been rejected by Byzantinists today. Such efforts generally require that we disfigure and distort east Rome to fit it into medieval western categories.[3]

Moreover, "feudalism" is a contested concept among western medievalists themselves, some of whom argue that it must be abandoned because it confuses rather than clarifies issues.[4] This makes the goal of integrating east Rome into the medieval paradigm of studies either undesirable (we do not want to take on the problems of other fields) or nebulous (on what terms will such an integration be accomplished?). Likewise, in Constantinople there was no effective separation of secular and spiritual powers, as the emperor remained in charge of religion, just as he had been in pagan times and in Christian late antiquity. Finally, Romanía was a properly consolidated state, with unified institutions under central control the likes of which did not exist in the west before the seventeenth or even the eighteenth century. Romanía did not experience anything like the slow growth of central state power that we see in the medieval and early modern west. The two paradigms just don't mesh. It would be a gross distortion to study the east Roman world through any of these supposedly signature "medieval" traits.

The fifth problem with a medieval rubric is its implication that the study of east Rome should be brought into closer alignment with that of Medieval Studies. It would imply that our field is a subfield of Medieval Studies, but the latter field is predominantly understood as focusing on western Europe,

---

3 See the nuanced remarks of Messis, "Byzance et l'Occident."

4 This is a long-standing debate; start with E. A. R. Brown, "The Tyranny of a Construct: Feudalism and Historians of Medieval Europe," *American Historical Review* 79 (1974): 1063–88.

and scholars who work on that material have their own separate conferences, periodicals, training, terms of art, and theoretical frameworks. In adopting their name for our field, would we be making a claim to belong to that group? Setting aside the issue of the theoretical terms on which such an alignment might take place, which I mentioned above, we would also face the practical problem of persuading medievalists to engage with our materials, a hurdle that I believe will be insurmountable. The vast majority of (western) medievalists are totally unwilling to engage with eastern materials—to say nothing of learning Greek. This would place us in an unequal relationship and force us into futile contortions in order to gain the attention of a different field that is not interested in our subject. This claim requires unpacking, as it involves a gap between ideals and practice in Medieval Studies.

There are medievalists who want to expand the narrow understanding of the Middle Ages that has long prevailed and that confines the field to western Europe. The overwhelming majority of research that is produced under the rubric of the Middle Ages focuses on western Europe, as is evident, for example, from the programs of the major medieval conferences (at Kalamazoo in the US and Leeds in the UK) and the books that are reviewed by *The Medieval Review*. After all, the field itself emerged from efforts by western nations to trace their own premodern origins. Medieval research in most countries focuses largely on what each country takes to be its own medieval past, with a thin layer of scholars on top whose work is transregional. An obvious exception to this pattern is research in Canada and the United States, which countries lack medieval phases. Another exception is Britain, where medieval research is more diverse than on the continent. But in general the priorities of research are structured by modern nationalities. Beyond the narrow silos that they create, the overarching medieval world to which they point mostly overlaps with western Europe and its colonial outposts.

Now, many laudable proposals have been made in favor of a "Global Middle Ages" that would expand the geographical and cultural boundaries of the field to encompass, well, a planetary scale in some instances, or else Byzantium, the Slavic and Islamic worlds, and Central Asia, depending on the goals and scale of each proposal. The relatively new ARC Humanities Press puts such an expansive vision of the Middle Ages into practice in its medieval series of publications, and there is now a Cambridge Elements series on the Global Middle Ages.[5] From a methodological point of view, there is much to recommend such an approach. It facilitates comparative work, reveals the interconnections of this broader world, and views its individual components (including western Europe) from interesting new perspectives. In many respects, it is an admirable approach. Many job searches reflect its priorities in what they claim to be seeking in applicants.

However, the Global Middle Ages has still not changed the fundamental biases of Medieval Studies, which remains stubbornly focused on western Europe and its colonial outposts. The intuitive and effective sense of "medievalist" is still someone who works on medieval western Europe. Such medievalists rarely attend the non-western panels at their own conferences, and it is even more rare for them to attend conferences on Byzantine, Slavic, or Islamic history. The problem stems from a stubborn lack of curiosity about those fields. It is quite easy to learn about them now, but most medievalist publications still reveal no knowledge about them. Many medievalists I have met candidly admit to me that they know nothing about Byzantine things, even if they work on monasticism or conceptions of empire, areas of inquiry where comparative study would benefit their inquiries. Some freely admit that they have no intention of delving into those fields and do not consider Greek, Slavic, Orthodox, or Arabic cultures to be a part of their own field. Others often admit their ignorance with an endearing sense of embarrassment, as if it were a minor vice that they *really* should do something about, you know, one of these days. Yet they never ask me

---

5 For a good introduction, see G. Heng, *The Global Middle Ages: An Introduction* (Cambridge: Cambridge University Press, 2021).

to recommend good introductory books. They can afford to be so blasé and good-natured about it because they know that it has no professional consequences for them. Their field is large and wealthy enough (in comparison to Byzantine Studies) to constitute its own separate and insular world of activity, and they can afford to ignore anything that goes on outside. They are perfectly aware that they don't need us, at least not in the current configuration of fields, and this state of affairs shows no sign of going away anytime soon. There is simply no way that medievalists will now start learning Greek, far less Slavonic and Arabic, and I would be surprised if many of them began to read those sources in translation.

Most introductory books, textbooks, and courses on the Middle Ages barely mention the eastern empire, if they include it at all, and those mentions are far less than the attention that it would merit simply in proportion to its geographic and demographic footprint. They do not represent it based on recent scholarship and often recycle old stereotypes. In sum, it remains to be seen whether the project of the Global Middle Ages will change these basic attitudes among many medievalists. The inertia, biases, ideological commitments, and professional identities that have traditionally marked Medieval Studies may continue to resist the rhetorical appeal and moral force of the "global." Therefore, if we adopted a medieval name we would be compromising the distinct identity and contours of our field and taking on the problems of a different field, without any prior guarantees that we would impact its practices and outlook and make it more inclusive of our own.

Before our field hitches its wagon to a "medieval" horse, we should first expect western medievalists to engage meaningfully with our work and the culture that we study. This would prove that a kind of merger is possible. But apart from a handful of cross-over giants (who have always existed), I see no proof that this is about to happen. It is therefore better for our field to maintain its own discrete identity and avoid becoming trapped in a frustrating and probably futile quest for recognition by medievalists. That would be an unequal partnership in which one side would just not be making the effort. At best, we would be a token "diversity" annex in a field that has more resources, personnel, and the backing of wealthier states than our own, and that has traditionally shown little interest in our sources and scholarship, even though the latter are readily available.

Moreover, beyond these issues of practice, the Global Middle Ages too is guilty of Eurocentrism, or intellectual colonialism, as it seeks to spread its own aspirational paradigm over the entire "globe," however the latter is defined. As an overarching paradigm for the coordination of many cultures, it would export the problems of the "medieval" to the rest of the world. But cultures other than those in western Europe had no "medieval" traits apart from simple contemporaneity; what they were going through at that same time was not necessarily "medieval." So why should they have to adapt to a rubric that stems from the particular history of western Europe? It is ethnocentric to expect them to, or to casually assume that "medieval" can function as some kind of "common" or "neutral" rubric for other cultures. Not for a second would western medievalists consider adopting period-labels from other cultures, assuming any "neutral" ones could be found!

Given the comparative power and wealth of western academic institutions and their expectation that everyone follow their own terminology—like BC and AD masquerading as BCE and CE—a "medieval" rubric may inevitably emerge as the only one that can facilitate discussion and exchange among all the otherwise separate fields that focus on this period. In other words, scholars of the caliphate, Romanía, and, say, the Mongols may just have to accept that the Global Middle Ages offers the best prospects for exchange and dialogue. Even so, this coordinating framework operates at a higher level than any individual field and makes no claim about what each of them should be named individually. The Global Middle Ages is more like a club of fields, each of which may retain its own identity and does not have to be explicitly pegged to the "medieval." The focus of this book is on what to call Byzantine

Studies, Byzantium, and the Byzantines, on their own. This should not include any variant of "medieval." Once we have found our own terms, we can then ask how our field, under a new name, might engage with the Global Middle Ages. One of its chief functions within that club of fields might even be to remind others of alternatives to the medieval in this period.

"New Romans"?

This label has a few points in its favor, most of them superficial, but ultimately it would cause too many problems. It stems from the second official name of Constantinople, i.e., New Rome. If we were to use it as an ethnonym, we would have a neat parallel between Rome and Romans (on the one hand) and New Rome and New Romans (on the other hand). This preserves the latter's Roman identity while signaling a transition into a new phase of Roman history. In addition, "new" has positive connotations, certainly compared to "late." This is partly why I used it in the title of my history, *The New Roman Empire*, borrowing the phrase from Edward Gibbon.[6] Besides ameliorating Gibbon's negative view of this phase of Roman history, the term gestures toward the renewal of the imperial tradition and its embarkation on a new trajectory. "Newness" can point away from decline and stagnation, with which Byzantium was long associated, and it also points to new ways of looking at it, in other words it is "seen anew." This was a literary choice for the title, and not a declaration about our subjects' identity.

At the same time, the terms "new" and "neo" can also point to a more ambiguous relationship to a canonical past, where the "new" lacks the authority of the old and yet still strives to live up to it, as we see in Neo-Latin and Neo-Hellenism (i.e., modern Greece and the modern Greeks). Even the medieval German empire is sometimes called a "Neo-Roman

---

6 Edward Gibbon, *History of the Decline and Fall of the Roman Empire*, ed. D. Womersley, 3 vols. (London: Penguin, 1994), chap. 13 (v. 1, 359: Diocletian; 390: Constantine).

empire," with the same implications. This too was an aspect of east Roman history, as it recursively looked back to and idealized past models such as Augustus and Constantine.

However, the eastern Romans never referred to themselves as New Romans, nor did they think of themselves that way, as distinct from just plain old Romans. Not even the residents of Constantinople called themselves New Romans, despite the City's designation as New Rome. I have found that term only in a legal commentary by Theodosios Zygomalas, who was writing in the late 1580s, about a century and a half after the fall of Constantinople. In glossing a Latin term, he notes that "the Romans call laws *leges*. The Romans are those who today are the Franks, while Greek-speakers [*Graikoi*, Zygomalas' people] are new Romans." This requires unpacking. In Greek texts that gloss Latin terms, "the Romans" means "Latin-speakers," so Zygomalas is saying that today's Latins-speakers are the western Europeans ("Franks"), whereas the Greek-speaking Romans (his own people) are "new Romans." This is fascinating, but is too late and too limited a basis on which to extend the term to the entire east Roman polity and its people. Zygomalas was writing at a time when his people had lost their Roman polity and when western Europeans, with whom he was in contact, were asserting powerful claims to the imperial tradition. As a result, his understanding of these terms does not align with those that had been used while Romanía still existed. For example, he seems to consider ancient Latin-speaking Romans as "Franks" too.[7]

It would be strange for us to call east Romans "New" during the entire millennium that their polity lasted after the foundation of Constantinople. For a while, there might have been something novel about a mostly Greek-speaking eastern empire with its own capital and with Christianity as its official religion. But that configuration was already old by

---

7 New Romans: S. Perentidis, *Théodose Zygomalas et sa Paraphrase de la Synopsis minor* (Athens: Sakkoulas, 1994), s.v. E 34; Franks: s.v. G 40 (under Marcus Aurelius).

the late fifth century, if not earlier. To keep calling its people "new" in the fifteenth century would be absurd. Moreover, there is a conceptual problem here too. Most of the big changes that contributed to the emergence of a distinct east Roman culture evolved over the course of generations or centuries. There was a continual process of adaptation, just as at ancient Rome. In a certain sense, *all* Romans in *any* period were New Romans, because Roman culture was always evolving. Thus, there was no point in history at which ancient Romans give way to people whom we can call New Romans in a categorical way.

To be sure, a cluster of developments around 300 AD accelerated the pace of change, including a new administrative and military system; the foundation of Constantinople; and the promotion of Christianity by the state and the creation of imperial Christianity. But most of these evolved over the course of a century or two and were not experienced as dramatic ruptures. Even the foundation of New Rome cannot function as such a rupture for us. There had been "new Romes" before it that set the stage for it,[8] and it took Constantinople itself a long time to become dominant as an imperial center and take on the mantle of "Rome" in its own right, even in the east. Rather than look for ruptures in order to justify our artificial sense that something essential changed, we need to learn to work with a large-scale timeline of Roman history where change is gradual.

Finally, there is a practical problem. It would be awkward to rename our field New Roman Studies. This is principally because the adjective New can, and certainly would, be taken to modify Studies (or Roman Studies), rather than the name Roman. In other words, most people would think that this was a new and revamped version of (ancient) Roman

---

8 A. Kaldellis, "How Was a 'New Rome' Even Thinkable? Premonitions of Constantinople and the Portability of Rome," in *Leadership and Community in Late Antiquity: Essays in Honour of Raymond Van Dam*, ed. Y. R. Kim and A. E. T. McLaughlin (Turnhout: Brepols, 2020) 221–47.

Studies, rather than a distinct field that studied New Romans. We should avoid courting that kind of ambiguity too.

"Romeans"?

"Romeans" is an Anglicized *phonetic* version of the standard Greek name for "Romans," Ῥωμαῖοι, which can be transliterated as *Rhomaioi* or *Romaioi*. Using this term would prioritize how the name sounded rather than what it meant. In Latin, the equivalent word is *Romani*, but the Greek version sounded something like *Roméi* (rhyming with, and bearing the same stress-accent as, "hey" or "hay"). Its adjectival form in English would be "Romean" or, better, *Romaic*, which is more faithful to the Greek adjectival form. I have heard this too proposed as an alternative to "Byzantine," and it is beginning to appear in print too. A recent sourcebook, for example, uses the transliterated form *Rhomaioi* far more often than it does the translated form "Romans."[9] The name of the field that this points to is Romaic Studies or Romean Studies.

   This option has attractive advantages, but also significant drawbacks that cause me to lean away from it. Specifically, it could be argued in favor of these terms that they are faithfully emic, that is, they were used by the people in question to refer to themselves. Thus, in using them we might avoid the accusation that we were still denying their identity, as our field has done from the start. Moreover, these terms are not used by other fields and so we could not confuse our subjects with the ancient Romans or the residents of medieval Rome. They also situate the Romeans within the tradition of Roman history while also acknowledging their distinctness as Greek-speaking Romans, for the term reflects the Greek version of the Roman name.

---

9 C. Rapp and J. Preiser-Kapeller, eds., *Mobility and Migration in Byzantium: A Sourcebook* (Vienna: Vienna University Press, 2023), used throughout.

But precisely therein lies the problem: these terms fail to acknowledge our subjects as fully Roman, and posit them instead as a kind of derivative, secondary, or qualified Roman-*ish* people. In reality, there is no point in history at which we can say that Roman history ends and Romaic history begins, largely for reasons that have already been mentioned: all the changes that brought about an allegedly distinct east Roman (or Romaic) culture were gradual, taking place over the course of centuries. Once we posit a different name for a later phase of the same culture, even if only for the sake of convention or convenience, scholars will rush to define the different "essence" of that later phase and postulate the factors that gave it a distinct identity. Scholarship really does work that way, because the human mind is easily tricked by mere names into postulating distinct essences. We will then charge down a rabbit hole to find the distinctive traits that separate the Romaic from the Roman, and forget the truth that there was only one Roman tradition, one Roman people, in continual evolution. John B. Bury made the point already in 1889: "No 'Byzantine empire' ever began to exist; the Roman empire did not come to an end until 1453...such expressions as Byzantine, Greek, or Romaic empire are highly objection-able, because they tend to obscure an important fact and perpetrate a serious error."[10]

It matters that there was no rupture between ancient Rome and Romanía, no "essential" departure from ancient Roman tradition, and that the ancient *and* medieval Greek term for the Romans was the same. For the sake of establishing an artificial scholarly distinction, we would be denying the basic lexical fact that in both antiquity and medieval times the term Ῥωμαῖοι referred to one and the same thing: the Roman people and their state, whether the latter was based in Rome or Constantinople. Furthermore, in modern Greek, which continues to use the same term, it would be impossible

---

10 J. B. Bury, *History of the Later Roman Empire from Arcadius to Irene (395 AD to 800 AD)* (New York: Macmillan, 1889), 1:v–vi.

to draw a distinction between Romans and Romeans, a telling realization from this standpoint. In other words, east Roman lexical usage posited identity and continuity from antiquity, and for us to break that in order to distinguish between Romans and Romeans perpetuates the cycle of denial and fake essences in which we have been trapped for centuries. It pedantically (and perhaps cynically) sticks to the letter in order to evade the obvious and intended spirit of east Roman usage of the common term.

Moreover, the "Romean" label is already heavily tainted by denialism. It has already been used often, in both medieval and modern times, in order to deny east Romanness, or it is otherwise implicated in that project. For example, it is well known that western medieval rulers, especially the German emperors, preferred not to recognize the eastern emperor as a Roman ruler of Roman subjects, and so they called him instead the "emperor of the Greeks," "emperor of Constantinople," "emperor of New Rome," or "emperor of Romanía," or (at worst) "king of the Greeks." These are all made-up alternatives to his correct title, which was emperor (or *basileus*) "of the Romans." Well, among these alternatives there sometimes appears this one: "emperor of the Romeans" (*imperator Romeorum* or *Romeon*, using the Greek genitive form in the Latin).[11] It was an underhanded way to be formally correct—at least *phonetically*—but still to engage in denialism, for *Romei* in western parlance did not mean anything, and certainly did not mean "Romans." If we were to use this term, it would effectively be to the same effect, because no one in the west

---

11 For these titles and their contexts, see E. Tounta, *Το δυτικό* sacrum imperium *και η βυζαντινή αυτοκρατορία: Ιδεολογικές τριβές και αλληλοεπιδράσεις στην ευρωπαϊκή πολιτική σκηνή του 12ου αιώνα (1135-1177)* (Athens: Ίδρυμα Ριζαρείου Εκκλησιαστικής Σχολής, 2008) 223-25, 399; A. Kolia-Dermitzaki, "Byzantium and the West—the West and Byzantium," in *Aureus: Volume Dedicated to Professor Evangelos K. Chryssos*, ed. T. Kolias et al. (Athens: National Hellenic Research Foundation, 2014) 357-80. I know additional instances from the thirteenth and fifteenth centuries.

knows, believes, or could easily be made to understand that these newly-discovered "Romeans" were just Romans. This would create confusion, and planned confusion is indistinguishable from obfuscation.

In the fifteenth century, we have the case of one Ioannes Kanaboutzes, a culturally Orthodox and Greek-speaking scholar who wrote a commentary on the *Roman Antiquities* of the ancient (Greek) historian Dionysios of Halikarnassos. Dionysios had famously argued that the ancient Romans were descended from the Greeks. In his commentary, Kanaboutzes draws a distinction between the *Romaioi* (his own people, in real time) and the *Romanoi* (derived from Latin *Romani*), who were the ancient Romans and possibly also the Latin-speaking "Romans" of his own time (who could also be called *Latinoi*). He implies that both were heirs of the ancient Roman tradition, making room for both Greeks and Latins under the same expansive umbrella.[12]

But the circumstances under which Kanaboutzes made this distinction argue against our adoption of it. Kanaboutzes was employed by, and writing this treatise for, a member of the Gattilusi family, the Genoese lords of a number of Aegean islands. Theirs was a colonial lordship that emerged in the aftermath of the Fourth Crusade, when western military and commercial interests dismembered the Roman polity and distributed its fragments among themselves to rule, subjugating the local population and relegating them to second-class legal status. These colonial lords did not recognize the identity of their Roman subjects and instead continued to call them "Greeks." Kanaboutzes, it seems, was trying to find some common ground between his own people (the *Romaioi*) and the Latins that could accommodate the claims of both to the Roman tradition. This is not a relationship that we should replicate in our scholarly practice. Adopting the Romaic term might be interpreted as begging for scraps or for an accom-

---

12 A. Kaldellis, *Byzantine Readings of Ancient Historians* (London: Routledge, 2015), 114, 118.

modation with our betters, to achieve which we have to compromise the stated identity of our subjects. The latter have the same claim to the Roman tradition, in fact a better one than anyone in the Middle Ages, and they should be recognized for that on equal terms with their ancient predecessors. They used the *Romean* label because they believed that they were *Romans*, which is what that word meant and still does mean in Greek, and not in order to set themselves into a qualified relationship with their own history.

A strand of modern Romanian national historiography, dating to the early nineteenth century, shows how the Romean-Romaic label lends itself to denialism. Most variations of the Romanian national narrative assert a strong continuity between the ancient Romans and the modern Romanians. Some of its exponents also sought to deny such continuity to the "Greeks," which is what the rulers and subjects of Constantinople supposedly "really" were, as proven by their use of the "Romaic" name instead of the Roman one.[13] Thus, a lexical quibble becomes the basis of ideologically motived denialism. I would caution against any label that suggested, even if only implicitly, that the east Romans were anything other than full Romans.

The Romean-Romaic label has a further disadvantage, which is that, unlike the terms "medieval Romans," "new Romans," and "east Romans," it can *never* shed its qualifier in order to allow our subjects to appear as just plain "Romans." It thus lacks the flexibility of the other, qualified terms. There are many contexts in which such qualifiers are not necessary, for example in specialized research, where it is clear which Romans are discussed and it is unnecessary to distinguish them at every turn from, say, ancient Romans. But the Romean-Romaic label would, in every context, irrevocably bar our subjects from appearing as Romans *tout court*. These labels would, moreover, force us to impose this artificial dis-

---

13 See the cases of Gheorghe Sincai and Petru Maior in D. Mishkova, *Rival Byzantiums: Empire and Identity in Southeastern Europe* (Cambridge: Cambridge University Press, 2023), 31–32.

continuity on Greek texts that otherwise refer to ancient and modern Romans through the same terms. The Greek tradition speaks with one voice about Romans, but we would have to modulate our terminology according to this artificial convention, and it would be unclear where to draw the line. Were Justinian and Prokopios Romans or Romeans? Or was one a Roman and the other a Romean, because of their respective native languages? Down this path lies more absurdity.

In my research I have found one context in which Romaic is appropriate and should be adopted as a formal category by scholarship. I mention it because changing the name of our field will have ripple-effects across many subfields and adjacent areas of research, and linguistics is one of them (this will come up again below, in our discussion of philology). Romaic was a name used by our Romans for the form of the Greek language that was *spoken* in Romanía, especially after ca. 1000. Linguistically, it differed little from modern Greek. The term "Hellenic" was increasingly reserved for the learned, ancient form, until at some point there emerged a quasi-formal distinction between Hellenic and Romaic as different kinds of Greek.[14] Scholars have struggled to name the form of Greek that was spoken at that time, repurposing western terms ("vernacular" and "vulgar") or terminology that emerged in modern Greece ("demotic").[15] Behind all this lies yet another form of Roman denialism. There is a studious pretense that there is no emic term for this form of the language, though experts must know that it was called Romaic

---

14 Kaldellis, *Romanland*, 97–106; and A. Kaldellis, "The Latinization of Greek in Byzantium and the Emergence of the 'Romaic' Language," in *Χρυσέαν φιάλαν*, Festschrift volume in honor of Ilias Anagnostakis, ed. M. Leontsini et al., forthcoming.

15 E.g., M. Jeffreys, "Modern Greek in the Eleventh Century—Or What Else Should We Call It?," *Kambos: Cambridge Papers in Modern Greek* 15 (2007): 61–89. D. Holton et al., *Cambridge Grammar of Medieval and Early Modern Greek* (Cambridge: Cambridge University Press, 2019) also never mentions the emic name for the language to which it otherwise devotes thousands of pages of analysis.

at least as early as the eleventh century and as late as the nineteenth. But the general imperative of Roman denialism has long placed all such terms off-limits. I propose that we use Romaic here. In the context of language, it does not de-Romanize our subjects, but quite the opposite. It shows that they extended their own ethnic label to their language, which they knew full well was "Greek" (or descended from it). The Romaic language was that spoken by the Romans, which in this period only happened to be Greek. In antiquity, it had been Latin.

"East Romans"

Whatever term we settle on, the discussion so far has demonstrated the utility of a term that has both a qualified form (X Romans), which will be used in contexts where it is necessary to distinguish our subjects from the ancient Romans and the medieval western Romans, and also an unqualified form (Romans), which reflects the natural usage of our sources and can be used by us when it is clear which Romans we are talking about. The latter category (unqualified form) includes the vast majority of usage in scholarship, except in the metadata (title or subtitle, the field- and journal-names, etc.). Alert readers have doubtlessly already discerned my thesis: the best option that we have at our disposal for the qualified form is the term "east Romans," which has an almost identical adjectival form. It works well in English and German (*Oströmische Zeitschrift* has a nice ring to it), though in French and Greek "Romans of the east" sounds better (*Romains d'Orient*; *Ρωμαίοι της ανατολής*).

"East Romans" is not chronologically qualified, and so it is not exclusive of, nor complementary with, the ancient Romans. This is good, because we *want* these two categories to overlap, in the way that ancient and medieval Romans cannot by definition. Ancient and east Romans did overlap; put differently, there were east Romans already in antiquity. Such figures of the first, second, and third centuries AD were early specimens of the distinctive configuration of cultural traits that became more prevalent fully later on. They include, for example, Josephus, a Jew who wrote in Greek to defend Scriptural history and obtained Roman citizenship, and whose works survive because they spoke to the interests of later Christian Romans; the general Tiberius Claudius Pompeianus, a native of Antioch who married a daughter of Marcus Aurelius and realized that Rome did not have to be only in Italy; the orator Ailios Aristeides, who held Roman citizenship and wrote in praise of Greek and Roman culture and his own personal savior god (Asklepios); and others. It is strange, unnecessary, and teleological to call these figures "proto-Byzantine." They were Romans of the east, who had a largely Greek culture but were no less Romans than their western counterparts at the time. I am tempted to push this category back to include the triumvir Mark Antony, who ruled the east Roman empire from Alexandria, transplanting almost the entirety of the Roman political machine (consuls, senate, armies, and courts) into the midst of a mostly Greek-speaking city. Thus, in abolishing the rubric "Byzantium" we would be replacing it with an alternative that encompasses the long history of Roman culture in the Greek, Jewish, and Syriac east. "East Roman" does this. Even in antiquity, east Rome was an ongoing process.

By the same token, "east Romans" allows us to recognize this group in the Ottoman empire too, as the name does not limit us chronologically. These were the descendants of the east Romans we study, living after the loss of their polity and surviving on as a distinct ethnic, religious, and linguistic group after 1453. They too face problems of visibility in scholarship. According to one misconception, the *Rum* ("Romans") of the Ottoman empire encompassed most Orthodox subjects of the sultans in a supra-ethnic configuration known as the "*millet* of Rum." These Romans, then, were a multiethnic religious community. But this approach is also complicit in Roman denialism, a western bias that renders us incapable of "seeing" Romans in the east. In reality, the Romans/*Rum* of the Ottoman empire were its Greek-speaking Orthodox subjects. They were regularly differentiated on ethnic grounds from other Orthodox groups, mainly the Serbs, Bulgarians, Vlachs, and Georgians. But because western scholarship cannot process their existence, it has insisted instead that the category Roman in the Ottoman empire included anyone who was Orthodox, following in this the *millet* system, which subordinated most Orthodox Churches in the empire to the patriarch of Constantinople. However, this grouping was effected late in the empire's history for technical administrative purposes and it never superseded or abolished the identities of the various ethnic groups. The Romans were one among those groups. They had a proper name of their own that we must learn to use, as all our sources from the Ottoman empire do.[16] As with the "proto-Byzantines" discussed above, it is equally strange and unhelpful to call them "post-Byzantines."

In sum, the rubric "east Rome" enables us to cope with long processes of gradual change, from the first to the nineteenth century, while respecting the identity of our subjects. East Rome first began to take shape among the Romans who settled in the east or native easterners who, as new Romans, were lifted up into the citizenship- and leadership-cadres of the ancient *imperium*. Then, for a millennium, east Romans constituted the surviving Roman polity in the east. Finally, they became subjects of another empire, the Ottoman. There were strong lines of continuity among the successive phases of this group. By looking at them in this way, we can extend east Roman history back into antiquity and forward

---

16 The scholarship on this is large and growing, though much of it still reflects western denialist bias or modern Greek nationalism. For an introductory orientation to what the sources actually say, see T. A. Kaplanis, "Antique Names and Self-Identification: *Hellenes*, *Graikoi*, and *Romaioi* from Late Byzantium to the Greek Nation-State," in *Re-Imagining the Past: Antiquity and Modern Greek Culture*, ed. D. Tziovas (Oxford: Oxford University Press, 2014), 81–97. For the *millet* system, see B. Braude, "Foundation Myths of the *Millet* System," in *Christians and Jews in the Ottoman Empire: The Functioning of a Plural Society*, ed. B. Braud and B. Lewis (New York: Holmes & Meier, 1982), 69–88.

into modernity, as indeed the evidence *requires* us to do. This cannot be done with the categories "medieval Romans" or "the Byzantines," or at least not without clumsy adjustments and distortions (on top of which we would still have to cope with the ideological problems of those terms). Remember that, in almost all specialized scholarship, these people need not be called *east* Romans at all but just plain Romans, which is what they were. The qualification is necessary only in contexts where this field of study needs to be differentiated from Roman studies in other areas.

One context in which ambiguity might arise is southern Italy, especially in the ninth to eleventh centuries. This region, which was ruled by officials sent from Constantinople, was complex in terms of ethnicity, religious practice, language, and political loyalties. Using "Roman" by itself can create ambiguity, because of the proximity of the city of Rome. Moreover, it is not clear that the local Greek-speakers identified predominantly as Romans rather than Greeks (*Graikoi*), which was the preferred term for them in the local Latin, Latinate, and Italian usage. In this context, then, the qualified term "east Roman" may be used in specialized research to distinguish those Romans who came to Italy from the Balkans, Asia Minor, or Constantinople.

It might be objected that the eastern label decenters our subjects and treats them as non-normative, in relation to a putative center that was presumably in the west. This is a problem that famously complicates the term Eastern Europe, for example. But it is not a problem for us, if we correctly understand the history of east and west in the Roman tradition. These labels were rooted in the history of the Roman empire and survived long after the western empire went extinct in the fifth century AD. Specifically, after 395 the Roman empire began to operate as two parallel, homologous, and sibling states. These were called by writers of that time the "eastern" and "western" Roman polities, and their citizens accordingly were the eastern Romans and western Romans. This terminology was used consistently, for example, by the eastern historians Priskos of Panion (in Thrace) and Malchos of Philadelpheia (modern Amman), in the fifth century. These qualifiers stopped being used after the fall of the western empire, but they were not forgotten. The east Romans remembered that they constituted only half of a former whole. In the sixth century, when the armies of Justinian returned to the west and attempted to restore the Roman empire there, some of them were aware that most of the western population (barring the barbarians who had ruled them in the meantime) were fellow Romans.

Even in later centuries, when the east Romans had dealings with the states of western Europe, and in particular with Rome, they could call themselves "east Romans" in their literature. When the emperors of the twelfth century married western brides, they flatteringly referred to them as descendants of the (ancient) western Romans.[17] In the debates over Church Union of the twelfth to fifteenth centuries, it was frequently noted by east Roman writers that the Greeks and the Latins had a common cultural and religious genealogy in the unified Roman empire of antiquity. Thus, after 395 AD the east–west polarity within the Roman tradition was not forgotten, authorizing us to use it as a field name.

When east Romans of the ninth century looked back to the earlier period, that is to the fourth and fifth centuries, they distinguished between east and west Romans in retrospect.[18] One domain in which this distinction remained alive was the

---

17 Sixth century: Belisarios in Prokopios, *Wars*, 3.16.3; cf. Marcellinus Comes, *Chronicle*, s.a. 508 AD, ed. and tr. B. Croke, *The Chronicle of Marcellinus* (Sydney: Australian Association for Byzantine Studies, 1995), who condemns the eastern emperor Anastasius' attack on the fellow Romans of Apulia. "East Romans" in later literature: Theodoros Prodromos, *Poem* 1.140, ed. W. Hörandner, *Theodoros Prodromos: Historische Gedichte* (Vienna: Österreichischen Akademie der Wissenschaften, 1974). Twelfth century: A. Kaldellis, *Hellenism in Byzantium: The Transformations of Greek Identity and the Reception of the Classical Tradition* (Cambridge: Cambridge University Press, 2007), 299.

18 E.g., in the *Synodikon Vetus*, 41.5, 64.2, 76.7, ed. and tr. J. M.

Church. As early as the fourth century, it became conventional to distinguish between eastern and western bishops, which was essentially a distinction between Greek- and Latin-speaking bishops. "Eastern" and "western" was how the two Churches were first distinguished, and then "Greek" and "Latin" based on their liturgical languages. This usage long antedated the terms Orthodox and Catholic, which possibly did not come into play for this purpose before the fifteenth century. The east–west distinction became so ingrained that the emperor Justinian (in the sixth century) pleaded that bishops stop calling each other eastern and western (or Greek- and Latin-speaking) because it created mentalities of opposition, whereas in truth they should be striving to be a single, unified Church (all taking orders from him, of course).[19] There was no "center" in this conception, only east and west.

The point is important, because it alleviates the fear that "east Roman" is a decentering, non-normative term. After all, this is the same reason why the West has historically called itself by that equally decentering label. It is common (and correct) to critique Eurocentrism and western supremacy, but it is rarely asked why the West calls itself by a term that also sets itself off-center. Most cultures situate themselves at the center of their known universe. The peculiarity of "the West" is something that we all know at an unconscious level, but often do not notice until someone points it out.

The West calls itself that precisely because of how the Roman empire split in the later fourth century. Just as the east Romans retained an implicit sense that theirs was only the eastern half of a once "global" empire, the people of western medieval Europe also continued to refer to themselves as "the West" and "the westerners," a usage that lived on pri-

Duffy and J. Parker, *The Synodicon Vetus* (Washington, DC: Dumbarton Oaks, 1979).

19 Justinian speaking through bishops that he sent to pope Vigilius: R. Price, *The Acts of the Council of Constantinople of 553* (Liverpool: Liverpool University Press, 2009), 1:211.

marily through their Church, as the western empire was long defunct. This West always implied a distinction from an east, which included the Greek-speaking Churches and the eastern empire. In the Middle Ages, "the West" was not a vague geographical term, as many scholars think. It was, in fact, the standard collective term used by the Christian cultures of medieval western Europe. Many medieval texts indicate that it was a fairly robust emic collective identity, with the "western Church" functioning in some contexts as an equivalent to what we would call the Catholic Church; with expressions such as "we westerners"; and even with authors who wrote "histories of the west."[20] It was not until the later fifteenth century that a switch occurred from "the West" to "Europe" as the collective term of choice, only to go back again to "the West" in the later nineteenth century.[21]

We cannot escape the striking conclusion that "the West" has called itself that because of a notional relationship to the eastern empire, a relationship that was embedded in its terminology and remains there still today. This was the case even after ca. 800 AD, when the west ceased to recognize the east as Roman and later wrote it out of the history of Europe, recasting it as a non-Roman oriental despotism. But in its conceptual genealogy, the term "West" retains always this notional tie to the eastern empire. Therefore, the proposed term "east Romans" partly restores balance and symmetry to east–west relations, and it finds support in the terminology used by people at the time. To be sure, the east Romans almost always called themselves Romans without qualification, and we should follow their lead in most contexts. But it is

---

20 Many of these expressions are documented throughout B. E. Whalen, *Dominion of God: Christendom and Apocalypse in the Middle Ages* (Cambridge, MA: Harvard University Press, 2009).

21 I. Walser-Bürgler, *Europe and Europeanness in Early Modern Latin Literature: "Fuitne Europa tunc unita?"* (Leiden: Brill, 2021); G. Varouxakis, "The Godfather of 'Occidentality': Auguste Comte and the Idea of 'the West'," *Modern Intellectual History* 16 (2019): 411–41.

not inaccurate, inappropriate, or Eurocentric to call them east Romans in discursive contexts that require us to distinguish them from other participants in the Roman tradition, whether the latter are ancient or western medieval, while still calling them Romans without any qualification in their own context. There was a tradition of eastern and western Romans lodged deeply in their own historical consciousness.

I tested this terminology at a conference held in May, 2023, at Dumbarton Oaks. My paper was on historiography and made the argument that east Roman histories were, in decisive respects, more like their ancient Roman counterparts than the ancient Greek ones; they used the latter more as literary models than for their conception of history. The proposed distinction between ancient and east Roman (i.e., Byzantine) historiography created no confusion, and happily allowed for cases of overlap, as explained above: Cassius Dio, for example, was a senator from the east in the third century AD who wrote a Roman history in Greek. At no point did I need to use the term "Byzantine," while the continuities between the ancient and the east Roman historical traditions were all the more apparent for not having to interpose that disruptive artificial term between them.

Finally, we may use the term "east Rome" in a general, collective sense, to refer to the entirety of the civilization, in place of "Byzantium." Rome in this sense does not refer to a city, as it does in the west. Constantinople was never called East Rome, so we may use the term to refer to the civilization as a whole. Precisely when Constantinople was being built, Roman writers were commenting on how "Rome" had ceased to be a city and had become a world, making in Latin the pun between *urbs* (city) and *orbis* (globe). As Roman citizenship had now become a universal attribute (within the boundaries of the Roman state), no place or person was more Roman than any other. The proper name Romanía emerged in the vernacular to capture this sprawling and diverse but unified world. In the east, the name "Rome" was sometimes used to evoke it too, and not used to denote only the city. The late tenth-century encyclopedia *Souda* gives, as one of the meanings of "Rome," that it was "the epitome of the world (*oikoumene*)." This *oikoumene*, in turn, referred to the whole Roman world, but rarely to places outside of it. We should not confuse it here with the modern term "ecumenical." For the east Romans, the *oikoumene* was nothing more or less than Romanía. They were reminded of this every time they heard the Nativity story in the Gospel, which says that Caesar Augustus decreed a census across the entire *oikoumene*.[22] Thus, just as the city of Rome was the epitome of the *oikoumene*, by late antiquity the *oikoumene* had become an extension of Rome, a Rome writ-large. East Rome was the world of the Romans of the east.

The proposal of this book, then, is that we use the following terms:

> *For the state and its society*: Romanía; the polity of the Romans (or Roman polity); the empire of the Romans (or Roman empire); and east Rome (the latter for purposes of disambiguation).

> *For the majority population*: Romans or east Romans (the latter for purposes of disambiguation).

> *For the field*: East Roman Studies.

This will not create confusion between ancient and east Roman studies, and will even allow for their overlap. But sharing the main noun-name is possible, just as ancient Greek and modern Greek studies are not confused. In most contexts, those two fields operate without qualifiers. For example, at Classics conferences or workshops on ancient history, references to Greek or Hellenic studies are taken automatically to refer to antiquity. At events that focus on modern immigration or monetary policy, references to Greece and

---

22 Luke 2:1; see A. Kaldellis, "Did the Byzantine Empire have 'Ecumenical' or 'Universal' Aspirations?," in *Ancient States and Infrastructural Power: Europe, Asia, and America*, ed. C. Ando and S. Richardson (Philadelphia: University of Pennsylvania Press, 2017), 272–300.

Greek studies automatically refer to the modern country and its people. In contexts where there might be ambiguity, the qualifier is added, with no difficulty. The same can happen with ancient and east Roman studies.

There will, then, no longer be "Byzantinists." What shall they be called? The answer, just as now, depends partly on what exactly they study. The same term may not be appropriate for those who study east Roman history, Orthodoxy, or the literature of this period, in the same way that "Byzantinist" was not always appropriate for some areas of study, at least not in some of their aspects. We will discuss them separately below. But for scholars who work mostly on the history of east Rome, whether political, military, social, cultural, or economic, the field-name should be no different from that of people who study ancient Greece or Rome: it would be east Roman historian, east Roman scholar, scholar of east Rome, and the like. We do not formally call historians of ancient Rome "Romanists" (a term that has many diverse meanings, which are mostly antiquated by now),[23] but historians of ancient Rome. So the answer to the question "What do you study?" could be "I study east Rome" or "the eastern Roman empire."

---

23 E.g., being Roman Catholic, working on the Romance languages, or specializing in Roman antiquities.

Chapter 3

Implications for Allied Fields

It is possible that not every former Byzantinist will want to identify as a scholar of east Rome. I am not referring here to unreconstructed denialists, but to historians who have a legitimate concern that the Roman paradigm does not capture the nature of their material (though it is likely that denialists will hide under that cover for a while). Specifically, this might include certain aspects of Orthodox history and identity and also of Greek philology (literature, paleography, and the like). We can imagine certain monks, for example, who gave up worldly things and traveled along international networks of Orthodox monasticism, paying little attention to the distinction between Roman and non-Roman. Let us assume that they could transcend their Roman ethnicity, even though others would still have continued to classify them by it. Still, many of them produced works of religious devotion and theology in which the word "Roman" never appears and the political and social context of their writing is invisible (which crucially, however, does not mean that it did not exist). Similar reservations might be expressed on behalf of people who had other concerns—local ones, or those relating to gender or occupation—that were not overtly related to issues foregrounded here. Why should they be placed under a Roman rubric, when a concern for such things was not foremost on their minds?

To a certain extent, this question misunderstands how field-names work in identifying and organizing research.

These names do not represent mentalities on a granular level, but cluster research into broad consortia. The same questions can, after all, be raised about the name of any field of historical research. Take ancient Greek studies, for example. Greek identity, or indeed any issue theorized overtly as "Greek," was only one interest among many for the people who are studied by that field, and a fairly abstract one at that. Field-names do not claim to represent what people were most concerned with on the ground. Rather, they operate at a high level of abstraction because their aim is to group research into thematic bundles and distinguish them from their peers, which are similarly bundled. It makes sense, then, for these bundles to be identified by a top-tier abstraction. It is possible, for example, that most people engaged in ancient religious rituals did not imagine, in so doing, that they were engaged in specifically *Greek* rituals (though some perhaps did). But it is still not illegitimate for us to call them that, seeing as our primary goal is to differentiate them from Roman, Persian, or Egyptian rituals.

In the same way, it is legitimate to subsume a wide range of the cultural sites that existed in the east Roman polity under a Roman rubric, even if their precise focus-points in people's lives was not overtly Roman-oriented. If the people in question were Romans of Romanía (whether in an ethnic, legal, or political sense), they were inevitably engaged with institutions that interfaced with those of the Roman state. This was true also of ecclesiastical and monastic institutions. This might be good enough for our purposes. What might prevent us from placing them under an east Roman rubric would be explicit avowals on our subjects' part that their activities were *not* to be understood as Roman. But this never happens (quite the contrary, as we will see below). In fact, most ways of life in Romanía, even some of the most Orthodox variety, were far more Roman-oriented than scholars have so far recognized, in large part because denialism has prevented the issue from being explored at all.

As discussed above, there were times when the east Romans called their language "Romaic" or "the tongue of the

Romans." Even though they knew that it was (what we call) Greek, they were Romans and that was their language, so this appellation made sense. Likewise, there were times when they called their religion "the Roman religion" or "the religion of the Romans," though primarily for them (as for us) it was labelled Christianity or Orthodoxy. The former usage, however, occurs in both secular and religious authors.[1] Remember that Christianity was the religion of the Romans because the Romans were ordered to be Christians by their emperors and they complied. In his edict of Thessalonike (380 AD), Theodosius I made it the law of the land that "the name Catholic Christian" should be reserved for those who agreed with him on theology, and he called this the *religio* that the apostle Peter transmitted "to the Romans."[2] This gives us a prima facie rationale for subsuming most aspects of east Roman life, including its religion, under an east Roman rubric.

But this does not solve our practical problems. The argument so far has focused primarily on the study of east Roman history, which deals with the Roman state and its population, the Romans. However, there are affiliated or allied fields – one might consider them subfields of Byzantine Studies—that examine aspects of this civilization that have other, established names of their own, such as the Greek language or Orthodox Christianity. How are they to interface with the east Roman rubric proposed here? Second, in some fields the term "Byzantine" is used in a specifically technical sense, which may, if we strip away the distorting frameworks of "Byzantium" and "the Byzantines," be retained for use in those highly restricted domains. And third, the Roman rubric does

---

1 E.g., Jerome, Letter 63.2 (the *fides Romana*); *Acta Conciliorum Oecumenicorum* 1.1.1, p. 112, ed. E. Schwartz (Berlin: de Guyter, 1927); *The Miracles of Saint Nikolaos*, ed. G. Anrich, *Hagios Nikolaos*, v. 1 (Leipzig: Teubner, 1913), 296; Corippus, *Iohannis*, 8.255–256; Prokopios, *Wars*, 6.6.19; Theophylaktos Simokattes, *History*, 2.3.5, 5.2.4, 5.3.4; Michael Attaleiates, *History*, 96.

2 *Codex Theodosianus* 16.1.2; for a translation, see C. Pharr, *The Theodosian Code* (Princeton: Princeton University Press, 1952), 440.

not cover all aspects of Orthodox life and identity in Romanía because the history of Christianity did not fully overlap with that of Romanía. It had its own trajectory and identity, and these only partly intersected with that of Rome. Moreover, Orthodoxy eventually extended beyond the boundaries of Romanía and became a world religion in its own right. Scholars of these developments have to be able to distinguish, at least analytically, between the Roman state and its official religion, and critically assess the degree to which they shaped each other. Similar arguments may be made for its literature and art. The following chapter will, therefore, consider the implications of our argument for the study of east Roman religion, art, and literature.

"Roman Orthodoxy"

The dominant religion of the east Romans, as opposed to the religions of the ancient Greeks and Romans, had an identity and name of its own, namely "Christianity" or "Orthodoxy." Christians attached great significance to the Christian name. Martyrs famously went to their deaths with the words "I am a Christian" on their lips. In internal Christian conflicts over doctrine, it was vitally important for each side to claim exclusive ownership of the Christian name and brand its opponents with other names which implied that they were not Christians but rather Arians, Nestorians, and the like. Thus, Christianity generated identities around its name in a way that no other ancient religion did.[3] The Roman polity also inspired devotion to a common name: this marked the ancient Romans and continued to do so even after their conversion to Christianity. To give a striking illustration, an imperial ambassador to the Persians in the sixth century assured them that the terms of a treaty would be kept: "You are making a treaty with *Romans*. It is enough to say 'Romans,' the name says it

---

3 For the issue of The Name, see Kaldellis, *New Roman Empire*, 72–75 (and passim).

all." An army officer put on trial in the same century for the murder of a foreign king is said to not deserve the name of a Roman. A treatise of the tenth century on the subject of war—the most quintessentially Roman activity—advises generals to embolden their men before battle by reminding them in rousing terms that they were Romans.[4] Many more such examples could be given.

Thus, Orthodox and Roman identities were not coterminous terms and, contrary to the claims made in the scholarship, did not overlap perfectly. During much of the twentieth century, when Roman denialism was taken for granted, it was common for scholars to assert that the essence of Byzantium was Orthodoxy, but now such claims make little sense. Orthodoxy could not possibly have been responsible for the values and institutions that deeply structured the east Roman political sphere, society, economy, and military, or even most of its laws. In most cases, Orthodoxy was plastered over these institutions in a symbolic but superficial way. Moreover, the two categories simply did not overlap, as people knew well at the time. There were Romans before Christianity existed, and even ordinary people in Romanía were acutely aware that these pagan Romans, their "ancestors," had persecuted the early Christians. Texts about martyrs were read out almost every day in church, and they usually identified the emperors who had done the killing.[5] Conversely, the east Romans were also aware that Orthodox people lived around them who were

---

4 Respectively: Menandros, *History*, fr. 6, here 6.1.30–32, ed. and tr. R. C. Blockley, *The History of Menander the Guardsman* (Liverpool: Francis Cairns, 1985), 54–55; Agathias, *History*, 4.4.1; and *On Skirmishing*, 23, ed. and tr. G. Dennis, *Three Byzantine Military Treatises* (Washington, DC: Dumbarton Oaks, 1985), 231. If we believe the east Roman historians, this was standard practice before battle.

5 C. Messis, "'Maximien' chez les martyrs: lectures du passé romain dans l'hagiographie byzantine," in *L'histoire comme elle se présentait dans l'hagiographie byzantine et médiévale*, ed. A. Lampadaridi et al. (Uppsala: Uppsala Universitet, 2022), 105–31.

not Romans, such as the Bulgarians, Serbs, Rus', and Georgians. The Romans considered them barbarians and looked down on them for that reason; their common faith failed to bridge the chasm that was created by ethnic-cultural chauvinism.[6] It was Roman identity that created these barriers with other Orthodox peoples.

Orthodoxy thus transcended Romanía, but its formative period was rooted in it so deeply that Orthodoxy generally cannot be studied without a knowledge of its east Roman phase. The same is true of many religions. Islam, for example, is still a product of the caliphate of the first centuries after the Arab conquests. But for our purposes there is a great difference between Orthodoxy and Islam. The former emerged within a preexisting state and society, the Roman one, was made to adapt to it, and was deeply shaped and formatted by it, to such an extent that historians speak of the Romanization of Christianity.[7] Orthodoxy did not create the Roman empire; rather, the opposite was true: the Roman emperors largely defined the forms under which Christianity prevailed thereafter. But this was not the case with Islam. It did not emerge within a preexisting state that coopted it and turned it to its own ends, as the emperors did with Christianity. It was Islam that provided the fundamental modes and orders of the caliphate that it itself created. The field is accordingly called Islamic Studies (or early Islamic), even when it refers to social, economic, political, and military history. In recognition of the fact that the vast majority of the caliphate's population was not Muslim, the term "Islamicate" is sometimes used in order to study its multi-faith society.

The point of this brief comparison is to highlight the importance of the preexisting Roman matrix for the creation of historical Orthodoxy. Romanía cannot simply be replaced with

---

6 A. Kaldellis, *Ethnography after Antiquity: Foreign Lands and People in Byzantine Literature* (Philadelphia: University of Pennsylvania Press, 2013), 126–39.

7 Heather, *Christendom*.

Orthodox identity, as so much twentieth-century scholarship wanted to do. But nor can the reverse be done. We need both labels for these two intertwined, but conceptually different fields of study. I have met many scholars who work on Orthodox material that is entirely "Byzantine" in time and place, but who resist the label of "Byzantinist" because they see themselves as scholars of the religion itself and not the historical state that housed it. Fortunately, we are well equipped with labels (and field-names) to cover the Christian side of the equation. The latter may be called Christian, Early Christian, Patristic, Orthodox, Orthodox Christian, Greek Orthodox, or Eastern Orthodox. The present proposal does not affect the use of these labels. But what shall we call the area of overlap between east Roman and Orthodox studies?

In the past, this was called "Byzantine Orthodoxy." For all the reasons that Byzantium is problematic in other contexts, it is problematic here too. Nor is it necessary. Churches in the Orthodox tradition are commonly named after their respective nations or states (e.g., Russian, Bulgarian, and Romanian), and so that can be done here too. For the phase or aspect of Orthodoxy that was distinctive to the east Roman world, we have little choice but to call it "Roman Orthodox."[8] This term is not otherwise in use by any other field and it forms a nice parallel and contrast to "Roman Catholic." Nor must it be qualified here as "east Roman," for Orthodoxy is already a term that is conventionally used for eastern (Chalcedonian) Christianity. Thus, in any context where one might be tempted to write Byzantine Orthodoxy, "Roman Orthodoxy" can be used instead.

Some scholars may be uncomfortable with this usage. Given how important Romanía was for the making of Orthodoxy, both for the east Romans themselves and for every other Orthodox Church since then, some may be tempted to

---

8 This usage has already been pioneered by N. Siniossoglou, *Radical Platonism in Byzantium: Illumination and Utopia in Gemistos Plethon* (Cambridge: Cambridge University Press, 2011), x and passim.

treat its east Roman phase as archetypal, as a kind of ahistorical Ur-Orthodoxy that was defined more theologically and less in connection with a specific state and society. The nebulous term "Byzantine" facilitated this approach, as it gestured away from the Roman state and Roman people to a vaguely broader concept, to the nebulous idea of a civilization-at-large, albeit one that never really existed. For example, Dimitri Obolensky's once-popular concept of the "Byzantine Commonwealth"—the continuum of Orthodox cultures that allegedly linked Byzantium to its Slavic neighbors—becomes impossible if we replace "Byzantine" with "Roman" or even with "east Roman." It would correspond to nothing in actual history; there simply was no "East Roman Commonwealth." His concept comes a bit more into focus if we call it what it is: the Eastern Orthodox (and mostly Slavic) Commonwealth.[9] Unfortunately, this concept is a modern fiction, in that it projects nineteenth- and twentieth-century concerns back onto the medieval past. At any rate, it is certainly clearer than any term that includes the vacuous notion "Byzantium."

In the end, it is impossible to extract the Orthodoxy of the east Romans from its Roman matrix. Only theologians, and not historians, may believe that an ideal-type of Orthodoxy existed somehow, somewhere during the east Roman millennium that was not at its core entangled with the Roman state and society. One Orthodox scholar has even proposed that Byzantium was not really Orthodox because Orthodoxy requires freedom of belief whereas what passed for Orthodoxy in Byzantium was a state-mandated and state-controlled religion.[10] Historians, however, must work with the only Orthodoxy that is available to us in the record, and for us that is the Orthodoxy that was mandated, regulated, and shaped from top to bottom by the Roman state. This Ortho-

---

9 D. Obolensky, *The Byzantine Commonwealth: Eastern Europe, 500–1453* (New York: Weidenfield & Nicholson, 1971).

10 C. Hovorum, *Political Orthodoxies: The Unorthodoxies of the Church Coerced* (Minneapolis: Fortress, 2019), 39–40, 44, 198.

doxy was Roman not only for that reason, or only because it emerged from the practice and belief of people who were legally or ethnically Roman. It was Roman for those reasons too, of course, but *also* because it was understood as Roman at the time.

There were moments when it was necessary for Orthodox Christians to specify that their religion was the Roman one. This happened because *all* varieties of Christianity consider themselves to be the One True Christianity and thus call themselves Orthodoxy (which means Correct Faith). Therefore, to identify his exact faith a Roman Christian could list the Ecumenical Councils that his Church accepted, or simply state that he was a Roman (or both). This is what the eleventh-century monastic reformer Nikon of the Black Mountain did in order to specify his religious affiliation when he found himself in the region near Antioch, where many "heresies" were mixed up together. His ethnicity became a way of specifying his religious affiliation: he was Roman Orthodox. The historian Attaleiates (also in the late eleventh century) had to do something similar when explaining how the Turkish conquest affected all the religious groups in the east. At first it was easy to attribute that misfortune to the heresies of the Nestorians and Monophysites, "but when disaster also struck the Orthodox, all those who followed the religion of the Romans were unsure what to make of it." When Roman authors wrote against the religion of the Armenians, they critiqued it for "breaking away from and dividing the Orthodoxy of the Romans."[11] Thus we see that when these Roman authors had to distinguish among *religious* groups on a macroscopic level, which is what our field-names also have to do, they used the Roman label to do so.

---

[11] Respectively: Nikon of the Black Mountain, *Taktikon,* prologue 20, ed. C. Hannick, *Das Taktikon des Nikon vom Schwarzen Berge* (Freiburg: Weiher, 2014), 34; Michel Attaleiates, *History,* 97; Euthymios of the Peribleptos monastery, *Against the Armenians,* in *Patrologia Graeca* 132:1201, 1216 (among many other instances that could be cited).

Some non-Roman authors did the same. Most Armenians, for example, belonged to a Church that did not accept the same Councils as did the Church of Constantinople. At a conference on doctrine in the twelfth century, one of them nevertheless declared that "I am a Roman," meaning that unlike other Armenians he accepted the Council of Chalcedon. When Armenians converted to the imperial Church, they were said to have "become Romans."[12] Therefore, in precisely the contexts that matter for our purposes—that is, for distinguishing among groups macroscopically, which is what field-names strive to do—"Roman" was used at the time to refer to what we have so far called Byzantine Orthodoxy. Yet the converse was not true: "Orthodoxy" by itself could not distinguish among the many groups who claimed that label, because everyone claimed to be Orthodox. In this case, we happen to have a recent proof-of-concept article. It examines east Roman views of Armenian religion and is entitled "East Roman Anti-Armenian Polemic, Ninth to Eleventh Centuries." Significantly, it is not called "Byzantine Anti-Armenian Polemic." It makes this change with no loss of historical specificity or intelligibility. Quite the contrary: "east Roman" is more specific and accurate than "Byzantine."[13]

Nor is there any reason to refer to a "Byzantine Church." What we have called that so far was really just the Church of Constantinople—or Church of New Rome—and its dependent suffragan and affiliated bishops. These were listed in documents known as *Notitia*. In other words, the imperial Church of New Rome was a specific institution with an identity of its

---

12 Respectively: Theorianos, *Disputation with the Armenian katholikos*, in *Patrologia Graeca* 133:148; Aristakes of Lastivert, *History* 23.159, tr. R. Bedrosian at https://archive.org/details/AristakesLastivertsisHistory. The Paulicians in the ninth century also used the ethnonym "Roman" to refer to the religious identity of the east Romans: Kaldellis, *Romanland*, 108.

13 T. Kolbaba, "East Roman Anti-Armenian Polemic, Ninth to Eleventh Centuries," *Journal of Orthodox Christian Studies* 3 (2020): 121–73.

own. There is no reason to call it "Byzantine." It was functionally a state Church. Prominent historians have called it a "national Church" with a "national character,"[14] also "the east Roman imperial church" and essentially a department of state.[15] This interpretation of the Church, while correct, is not necessary for our purposes, but it further recommends that we identify the imperial Church with the name of the polity to which it belonged and no longer as "Byzantine."

The Romanness of Orthodoxy was not just a matter of names and labels. It cut to the heart of what religion *did* in Romanía, in a host of contexts. This is not the place to provide a full discussion with references, only to gesture at the deep connections between Roman identity (verging on what we would call patriotism) and Orthodox practice and belief. Church services in Romanía routinely ended with prayers on behalf of the emperor and the court, asking for military victories over the barbarians. Religious gatherings and processions in Constantinople, as documented in detail in the *Book of Ceremonies*, engaged the palace, the people of the City, and the clergy in prayers and acclamations to the same effect. The emperors were the effective heads of the Church, regulating it in all respects, making (or vetoing) episcopal appointments, and often deciding on its doctrines, internal

---

14 Respectively: P. Charanis, "On the Question of the Evolution of the Byzantine Church into a National Greek Church," *Βυζαντιακά* 2 (1982): 95–109, here 102; and P. Magdalino, "Enlightenment and Repression in Twelfth-Century Byzantium: The Evidence of the Canonists," in *Το Βυζάντιο κατά τον 12ο αιώνα: Κανονικό δίκαιο, κράτος και κοινωνία*, ed. N. Oikonomides (Athens: Εταιρεία βυζαντινών και μεταβυζαντινών μελετών, 1991) 357–73, here 371.

15 Respectively: L. Brubaker and J. Haldon, *Byzantium in the Iconoclast Era (ca 680–850): A History* (Cambridge: Cambridge University Press, 2011), 16; R. Macrides, "Nomos and Kanon on Paper and in Court," in *Church and People in Byzantium*, ed. R. Morris (Birmingham: Centre for Byzantine, Ottoman and Modern Greek Studies, University of Birmingham, 1990), 61–86, here 61.

rules, and practices. Even some saints' lives ended with prayers for the emperors and, when it came to describing war with barbarians, exhibit an "us versus them" mentality, even when the enemy was also Orthodox (for example, the Bulgarians). It is safe to call these texts "east Roman hagiography." There was no "Commonwealth" and no "ecumenical Orthodoxy" in these texts, only Roman patriotism infused with religious fervor.

In conclusion, there are contexts in which it is safe and appropriate to speak of Orthodoxy generically, perhaps even in a transhistorical or transnational sense, for Orthodoxy could "travel" and create devotional cultures that crossed polities. But wherever our field used to speak of "Byzantine Orthodoxy" more specifically, it is now better to call that "Roman Orthodoxy." It was understood that way by the Romans themselves and by some of their neighbors. The concept is not only appropriate but necessary.

Art History

It may prove harder for art historians to dispense with the term Byzantine. Political and social historians can advance to an east Roman paradigm and expect their colleagues and the public at large to catch on; in fact, their field might emerge from this change with enhanced prospects and visibility. But art historians do not have an obvious and viable alternative, and their field has invested the term Byzantine with associations that have paid off, especially in the study of icons and religious iconography. There is no clear replacement at hand. "East Roman icons" does not sound quite right (or as alluring), and it fails to evoke the defining religious dimension that undergirds the study of icons. Thus, a separate discussion is warranted, as the conventions and concerns of art history are distinct from those of Byzantine history and philology.

Byzantine art history originated in a different set of concerns than animated the study of history and philology. A major role in its formation was played by the rediscovery of Byzantium in late-nineteenth century imperial Russia, in particular the rediscovery of religious icons as a link between Byzantium and Russia. Icons could also be seen as the link between east and west, and a debate raged around the turn of the century about whether Byzantine art was more influenced by the orient (and was therefore "oriental") or was an organic offshoot of classical art (and therefore was credibly "western"). We need not get into the details of these debates here. They are important, among other reasons, for positioning Byzantine art—especially icons—within sweeping trajectories of long-term artistic evolution, from the ancient Near East to the later Roman empire and from there to medieval western Europe (on the one hand) and to Russia and the broader Orthodox world (on the other). Therefore, in art history "Byzantium" refers not only to a specific society and state, but also to a nexus of broader stylistic concerns that stands at the intersection of larger trajectories, from antiquity to the present and between east and west. This makes it harder to take a narrowly east Roman approach to it. It is harder not necessarily because of the material itself, but because of the narratives and theoretical concerns that have been built around it, including the cross-cultural debates about iconicity and figural representation in which the field is invested.

Despite these broad theoretical concerns, it is nevertheless possible to chip away at the problem starting at the ground level, as it were, in order to isolate the terminological stakes. After all, Byzantine art history is only predominantly about icons and iconography, not exclusively so. Let us look at everything else first, for instance imperial art and architecture, along with all other secular art and architecture, including many mosaics (those, at least, that are not religious icons). There is also the art of daily life and material culture, for example fabrics (clothing, curtains, etc.), bowls and other ceramics, and many illuminated manuscripts. These objects are receiving increasing attention from scholars, and there is no good reason to call any of this material "Byzantine." It is just east Roman art and should be so labeled, with no complications. None of this material is implicated in cross-cultural theoretical debates, where its standing and visibility to other fields might depend on wearing a "Byzantine" mask. I cite here some indicative studies of this material, all of which use "Byzantine" or "Byzantium" in the title, but where these terms can easily be swapped out for the real name.[16] The same is true of the east Roman reception of classical art, especially statues, which stood in the streets and on the monuments of Constantinople and other cities by the hundreds. Insofar as these impacted artistic trends and perceptions, they did so in ways that were distinctively east Roman.[17]

The same argument can be made for east Roman architecture, and not just for secular buildings. Architecturally, so-called Byzantine churches emerged from the ancient Roman basilica form. They developed that form in different directions later on, but the following observations justify calling them east Roman churches, not Byzantine. First, at any time in the long history of Romanía the architectural forms of most churches were relatively coherent and consistent. This is not to deny variations or regional differentiations, but at any time the plans and styles were generally recognizable. "There is a common vocabulary of architectural sculpture

---

16 Indicative publications: H. Maguire and E. Dauterman Maguire, *Other Icons: Art and Power in Byzantine Secular Culture* (Princeton: Princeton University Press, 2007); K. Dark, ed., *Secular Buildings and the Archaeology of Everyday Life in the Byzantine Empire* (Oxford: Oxbow Books, 2004); K. Dark, *Byzantine Pottery* (Stroud: Tempus, 2001); A. Walker, *The Emperor and the World: Exotic Elements and the Imaging of Middle Byzantine Imperial Power, Ninth to Thirteenth Century C.E.* (Cambridge: Cambridge University Press, 2012); E. Boeck, *Imagining the Byzantine Past: The Perception of History in the Illustrated Manuscript of Skylitzes and Manasses* (Cambridge: Cambridge University Press, 2015).

17 P. Chatterjee, *Between the Pagan Past and Christian Present in Byzantine Visual Culture: Statues in Constantinople, 4th–13th Centuries CE* (Cambridge: Cambridge University Press, 2022); P. Stephenson, *The Serpent Column: A Cultural Biography* (Oxford: Oxford University Press, 2016).

between Skripou, Asia Minor and Constantinople...whether or not the sculptors were local or from Asia Minor."[18]

Second, while allowing for cross-cultural influences in all directions, east Roman churches as a group were distinct from Armenian, Georgian, Serbian, and Rus' churches, to mention a few neighboring traditions of church building. The case of Bulgaria is more complex, because the Bulgarians lived directly next to Romanía in lands that already had native Roman traditions of church building; they received Orthodoxy from Romanía relatively early; and also because Bulgaria was militarily occupied by the Romans for almost two centuries (1018–1185). As a result, Bulgarian churches of this period resemble Roman ones.[19] But in the case of the other groups mentioned above, experts can tell them apart and so could people at the time. It is their distinctive traits that enable experts to write separate studies of Byzantine architecture in the first place. So if we can talk about Armenian, Georgian, Serbian, and Rus' churches, we should also be able to talk about east Roman churches too. We gain nothing by putting them behind a Byzantine label. The other building traditions are named after the groups or states that built them, as is standard practice in scholarship when distinct styles like these emerge. The sole exception is the east Romans, because western historiography has refused, for ideological reasons, to recognize the existence of these Romans. This perpetuates the bias that all other people have their own identities, ethnicities, and distinctive styles except for east Romans, who have so far been a "non-group" in the western view. But we can now acknowledge that these Romans were a real people with distinctive building traditions. It is time for our scholarship to recognize them as such.

---

18 R. Cormack, "Away from the Centre: 'Provincial' Art in the 9th Century," in *Byzantium in the Ninth Century; Dead or Alive?*, L. Brubaker (Aldershot: Ashgate, 1998) 151–63, here 154.

19 Cf. C. Mango, *Byzantine Architecture* (New York: Rizzoli, 1985), 168–75.

We come, finally, to the difficult issue of icons. These are defined broadly, as any pictorial representation of Christ, the Virgin, and the saints, in any medium, ranging from wooden panels and mosaics to vast painted programs on the walls of churches. The emphasis in research is on icons that were used during worship and on the theories that were developed to explain and justify this practice. It is to these religious icons that Byzantine art history owes much of its visibility and success, which have been considerable. To be sure, a great deal is owed also to architecture, with monuments such as Hagia Sophia adding luster to the field, but building traditions can easily be relabeled as east Roman or Roman Orthodox. It is not so easy in the case of icons, which scholarship situates within long traditions of figurative representation that bridges cultures and has ancient roots and modern extensions.

We need to be clear that there is a lot at stake here. Byzantine art history is the most successful of the all the fields that make up Byzantine Studies, measured for example in terms of persuading departments of art history that their field is necessary. To be sure, many art historians lament the lack of academic positions in their field, but even so it is in a vastly better position than all the other branches of Byzantine Studies. At the annual meetings of the Byzantine Studies Conference (of North America), typically about half the papers are given by art historians, which is not a distribution one sees in most other historical fields. Historians have had far less success in persuading their departments that Byzantine history is necessary. Philologists have probably had the least success. There are only a few positions for them outside of Greece, where there are obvious national priorities at work, given the importance of language for modern Greek identity.

If Byzantine art history enjoys a slightly better position, it is in part due to the prominence that icons have gained in broader debates within art history about figural representation and religious devotion. It has little to do with imperial or secular art, or even the fine arts, except insofar as they feature icons or are icon-adjacent. Byzantine art historians have generated significant dividends for their field by capitalizing on the fact that their culture is emblematic of icons in general, an association they have successfully cultivated. Moreover, that culture did not just produce and venerate icons, it also theorized their veneration in long philosophical texts, in response to Iconoclasm. Thus, it generated a significant and sophisticated body of pro-icon theory that can be used to engage productively with modern art historical theory, a feat that is rare for any premodern society. Art historians have successfully deployed Byzantine iconophile theory in modern debates about images and representation. In addition, they have produced models for studying "the power of images" and analyzing icons across cultural divides and in diachronic ways. This field spans from antiquity to the present, and encompasses many world religions. Thus, Byzantium is central or at least important to these debates.

The field has, therefore, nailed its colors to an explicitly "Byzantine" mast. All this theoretical capital, which continues to pay dividends to the field, has been branded as Byzantine, and it is not clear whether this name can be changed—or to what. Everything else with which the field deals can be relabeled as east Roman or Roman Orthodox, but I confess that I have no easy solution to this conundrum. Ultimately, this is a question that art historians will have to resolve for themselves. Do their methodologies and debates *require* the term Byzantine? Is their "brand" within art history tied to the rubric "Byzantine"? If so, there may be something problematic lodged there, at the very core. It results in strange discussions where art historians wrestle with the fruitless question of what exactly is "Byzantine" in "Byzantine art." Here, a problematic and made-up modern concept is driving the research agenda. But perhaps we can define the problem in a more precise way and thereby point to a path forward.

As a term of art, Byzantine iconicity wants to transcend its east Roman context and speak for traditions of representation that crossed cultures and defy periodization. Yet by branding itself as "Byzantine" it fails to escape its origin in the art forms and theoretical concerns that emerged in one particular historical society, Romanía. Consider the problematic term "post-Byzantine," which is used by scholars for art in the Balkans and elsewhere after the fall of Constantinople. It reveals a failure of nerve in this regard. The Byzantine state no longer existed and, after 1453, no field of scholarship refers to "the Byzantines." Why should the art of these people, then, be labeled as "post-Byzantine"? Moreover, this ambiguous term is applied to the religious art of many traditions, not just that of the Greek Orthodox Church. What we have here is a term that wants to break free from its moorings in east Roman history and become a free *stylistic* signifier. Perhaps we should help it do so. The term "Byzantine" can be retained if we define it purely as a stylistic label and use it only as an adjective. In other words, "Byzantine" in art history would refer to a kind of iconicity, wherever and whenever it appears, and it would not require or even imply the existence of anything called Byzantium or the Byzantines. Art historians, like all other scholars, would not refer to such entities. Thus, there would be no such thing as "post-Byzantine" art. There would be only Byzantine-style icons in the Ottoman empire, just as there was Byzantine-style art in Russia and (why not?) Byzantine-style art in east Rome. The term Byzantine might then capture the visual and stylistic koine that linked east Roman art to its "affiliated" cultures, as was recently shown by the magnificent exhibition at the Met in New York on Africa and Byzantium. Labels drawn from the particular legal, political, ethnic, linguistic, and even religious identities of the relevant groups do not capture the broader stylistic interconnections at work here.[20]

I confess that even this solution, in reality a concession, leaves me troubled. We still have to reckon with the connotations of the word. It would be a shame if this concession became a back door by which all the exotic, mystical, luxuri-

---

20 A. Myers Achi, *Africa and Byzantium* (New York: The Metropolitan Museum of Art, 2023).

ous, "spiritual," and decadent images of Byzantium sneaked back in. To be sure, those associations sell tickets to museum exhibitions of atmospherically illuminated icons, but they sell our subjects short. Romanía and its religious culture was no more exotic, mystical, luxurious, spiritual, or decadent than any other. It is only orientalism that has made it seem so, serving up alluring oriental alternatives to drab modernity.

As this is an issue for art historians to work out, I limit myself to some concluding remarks. Perhaps the labels "east Roman" or "Roman Orthodox" cannot reproduce the functions that "Byzantine" performs in the brand identity of Byzantine art history. Nevertheless, the veneration of icons in Orthodox Romanía had deep roots in the religious cultures of the ancient Roman empire.[21] Moreover, the central argument advanced by iconophile theologians in defense of the veneration of icons relied overtly on an argument made in antiquity about the legal ontology of Roman imperial images. Specifically, while the emperor was physically absent from most locations, his images could, for legal purposes, be regarded as if they were the emperor himself. Appeals passed via the image to the emperor himself. This notion provided the basic template for the interpretation of icon-veneration, which was regarded as passing through the image to its archetype. Thus, the theoretical justification of icon-veneration in Orthodox culture emerged from the matrix of Roman legal thought and practice.[22]

Finally, whether or not a new rubric is devised for the discussion of icons, there is no reason whatever for Iconoclasm

---

21 T. F. Mathews, with N. E. Muller, *The Dawn of Christian Art in Panel Paintings and Icons* (Los Angeles: Getty Publications, 2016), with the corrections, and a more regional approach, in P. Niewöhner, "The Significance of the Cross Before, During, and After Iconoclasm," *Dumbarton Oaks Papers* 74 (2020): 186–242.

22 A. Kaldellis, "Roman Quasity: A Matrix of Byzantine Thought and History," in *The Oxford Handbook of Roman Philosophy*, ed. M. Garani et al. (Oxford: Oxford University Press, 2023), 548–67, here 553–54.

specifically to ever be called Byzantine again. Iconoclasm was a movement by some emperors in the eighth and ninth centuries to limit and then abolish the use of icons in religious worship. It was eventually overturned by other emperors, who normalized their use, and a number of writers produced detailed technical treatises explaining why this was not idolatry. The Orthodox Church subsequently condemned iconoclasm and affirms icons as part of its core identity. But these events were highly distinctive features of east Roman history.

Iconoclasm occupies a prominent position in the brand identity of Byzantine art history, because it was a moment when images became a burning political issue. It turned art history into general history, which happens rarely. Yet whatever that movement was exactly about, it was an east Roman matter through and through. It isolated Romanía from other Churches that otherwise shared the same creedal confession, including Rome and Palestine. This isolation was the reason given by the empress Eirene for ending the first phase of Iconoclasm in 787, and it likely motivated the empress Theodora to do so again in 843, after the second phase.[23] Christians living elsewhere went through their own versions of Iconoclasm—for example, in Armenia, Palestine, and Francia—but they were all different affairs, much more limited and with different concerns and outcomes. The one that we call Byzantine Iconoclasm was specifically a chapter in east Roman religious history, limited to Romans. We do not even have to qualify it as *east* Roman, as there was no other episode like it in all of Roman history. Therefore, much of this history of icons, ranging from their ancient roots to the controversies and theories that they generated, turns out to have been specifically Roman in nature.

---

23 Kaldellis, *New Roman Empire*, 467.

Literature and Philology

If Byzantine art has built up brand-name recognition, Byzantine literature has none, at least among non-experts. While most of its important texts have been translated, none are widely recognized, studied, or read. Athanasios' *Life of Antony* might be assigned in courses on early Christianity and monasticism, and Prokopios' *Secret History* occasionally appears in courses on later Roman history. Readers who are personally invested in Orthodoxy read theological or gnomic literature. Beyond that, knowledge of secular Byzantine texts outside academia is virtually nil, and there are currently no prospects that this will change. A major reason is that our scholarship, for all of its undeniable advances in many areas, has not yet made the case (a) that these texts are enjoyable to read, or why (indeed, it is not clear that most experts enjoy reading them), or (b) that these texts speak to concerns that transcend the circumstances and ideologies of the authors who wrote them. There are exceptions to this pattern,[24] which hopefully will gain traction, but the field is too conservative and narrow in its outlook to offer much ground for optimism. For Byzantine texts to make the leap from expert analyses to popular appreciation, an entirely new framework for their study needs to be built. I see no signs of that happening presently.

In large part, this is because Byzantine texts are rarely studied as literature to begin with. They are instead the subject-matter of *philology*. Long ago, in the days of European humanism, philology referred to the love of the written word, of style, argument, and any form of artful communication. It used to have a broad remit, encompassing all that we would call the humanities, and even the arts and

---

24 E.g., A. Goldwyn, *Witness Literature in Byzantium: Narrating Slaves, Prisoners, and Refugees* (Cham: Palgrave Macmillan, 2021); E. Kefala, *The Conquered: Byzantium and America on the Cusp of Modernity* (Washington, DC: Dumbarton Oaks, 2020).

sciences.[25] But in Byzantine Studies today it is understood narrowly, mostly as editions of texts, commentaries, paleography, and linguistic analysis. It can extend as a far genre-analysis. These are necessary technical skills for the survival and future of the field. But it is wrong to believe that they are the heart and soul of philology. Literary approaches are more common in the US and UK, but there are few positions there. There are more positions in continental Europe, especially in Greece, where Byzantine texts form part of the national patrimony, though the approach to them is, for the most part, narrowly philological. It is so narrow that many institutions expect a new critical edition of a text from the manuscripts in order for someone to even qualify as a philologist. This results in the publication of many trivial texts, while major texts and authors are receiving scant interpretive attention.

Astonishingly, translating Byzantine texts into modern languages does not count as "real" philological work. As I have made translations myself, including of texts where hardened philologists fear to tread, I have occasionally asked about this. However, I have never received an answer coherent enough to reproduce here in credible form. Something about translation being "popularizing" or not based in an examination of the manuscripts. Yet in philology departments, colleagues down the hall who work on ancient literature in the same departments are not expected to work with manuscripts or prepare new editions, while, at the other end of the hall, philologists of modern Greek mostly work with printed books. Moreover, a case can be made that translating a text may require a closer engagement with its grammar and meaning than does editing it from a manuscript. I am not convinced that being able to transcribe and even correct the grammatical mistakes in a text proves that one understands what it is saying or even what any particular sentence means.

---

25 J. Turner, *Philology: The Forgotten Origins of the Modern Humanities* (Princeton: Princeton University Press, 2014).

At any rate, the remit of Byzantine philology does not include addressing other fields to make the case for the literary merits of our texts.[26]

Academic philology organizes texts and corpora by language, not history, cultural affinity, or logic. Byzantine philology is thus a subset of Greek philology, encompassing its "medieval" phase. Conventionally the category includes all Greek texts written roughly between 330 and 1453. At the University of Athens this is classified as "Byzantine philology," whereas at the University of Thessalonike it is "medieval Greek philology." Yet the e-journal published by the latter department is called *Parekbolai: An Electronic Journal for Byzantine Literature*. It is the only journal I know that is exclusively dedicated to this topic (though all Byzantine journals devote coverage to analyses of texts, whether philological or literary in approach).

How might this field adjust to the removal of the term "Byzantine," if in other contexts it were replaced with "east Roman"? From an Anglo-American, cultural-studies perspective, it would make sense to relabel its subject-matter as east Roman literature, and to place the burden of analysis on the "literature" side. What exactly was literary about these texts? How are they intellectually stimulating? Do they have anything meaningful or interesting to say to us today? But scholars who are on the more philological side of things would be more likely to see the same texts as constituting the textual corpus of medieval Greek. Modern linguistic categories here take priority over the identity of our subjects, yielding a field-name like medieval Greek philology or medieval Greek litera-

---

26 There are some rare wonderful exceptions, though their impact is probably bound to be limited; see M. Detoraki, "Γιατί το Βυζάντιο στη μέση εκπαίδευση," in *Συζητάμε για την εκπαίδευση: Δυσκολίες, προκλήσεις, προοπτικές*, ed. A. Kastrinaki and E. Katsarou (Rethymno: Philosophical School of the University of Crete, 2021) 80–92, which was also published (in modified form) in a major newspaper.

ture. But more hinges on the distinction between east Roman and medieval Greek than appears at first.

The society of east Rome was not monolingual. Sticking here only to languages that were used for writing, in the early period (fourth to seventh centuries) we also have Latin, Syriac, Coptic, Hebrew, and Gothic (though little survives of the latter). Many texts in these languages were written at the same time and in the same places as their Greek counterparts, often side-by-side. They reflect similar concerns, adhere to similar conventions of genre, and many were translated from one language into another. For example, just in sixth-century Constantinople historiography was produced in Greek, Latin, and Syriac; hagiography was written in Greek and Syriac; and law was issued in Latin and Greek. But our linguistic approach artificially silos these texts into separate compartments—and separate academic departments. Moreover, there is a classicist bias here that places Greek and Latin together, often in the same department, as prestige languages of the European tradition, while segregating them from the "oriental" languages, such as Coptic and Syriac. But in some places or periods, Greek was more fully engaged with those languages than with Latin.[27]

To be fair, philologists of Greek and Latin are not the only ones who isolate their material and make it seem exclusive. The study of Jewish texts of this period is even more walled off from surrounding languages and fields, adopting a highly esoteric and inaccessible style. As for the study of Syriac texts of this period, it is more accessible but is obsessively focused on Christian identity issues, paying little attention to the common social and political context that Syriac authors shared with their Greek counterparts who were writing at the same time in the same cities. I will illustrate this with an

---

27 A. Papaconstantinou, "Byzantine and Western Narratives: A Dialogue of Empires," in *Is Byzantine Studies a Colonialist Discipline? Toward a Critical Historiography*, ed. B. Anderson and M. Ivanova (University Park: Penn State University Press, 2023) 111–20, here 112–13.

anecdote. A former student submitted an article to a leading journal in Syriac studies, and one of the peer reviews challenged him to prove that his authors knew that they lived in the Roman empire. This reflects more on that field than on the Syriac east Roman authors themselves.

So how are we to define the field here? Is there "a" field here at all? From a cultural-studies and literary approach, i.e., one that is not strictly linguistic, it makes more sense to take a holistic approach and declare this field to encompass all the texts produced by the east Romans, or by the subjects of the eastern empire, regardless of what language they used. While I can appreciate the appeal of narrow linguistic expertise, as my expertise is primarily in Greek, it also inculcates blind spots and then naturalizes them. But the divisions imposed by linguistic approaches do not reflect how east Roman society operated or how literature was produced and consumed. Instead, it reproduces the conveniences of our academic disciplines. The literature of a diverse empire should not be defined in such narrow, artificial terms.

This pertains not only to the early period but the middle and late ones too, though the dynamics were different. Granted, Romanía was more monolingually Greek in those periods, however during its maximal imperial expansion (tenth and eleventh centuries) it ruled over subjects who wrote in Latin, Hebrew, Armenian, Arabic, and Bulgarian. The empire reached from southern Italy to the Caucasus. Yet works in those other languages never appear in surveys of Byzantine literature from this period. They are not even mentioned, far less studied in tandem with the Greek ones.[28] Granted, at the time "Romans" were understood to be one specific ethnic group among the rest, namely the dominant Greek-speaking one, though a more inclusive legal-politi-

---

28 It remains to be seen whether studies such as A. M. Robert's *Reason and Revelation in Byzantine Antioch: The Christian Translation Program of Abdallah ibn al-Fadl* (Oakland: University of California Press, 2020), will impact the theorization of "Byzantine literature" for that period or more generally.

cal definition of Romanness also operated in parallel to the more narrow ethnic one. Based on that more inclusive view, and the fact that Romans ruled over others in a context of empire, an "east Roman" rubric can more effectively bring them all into constructive dialogue under one roof, a feat that is impossible for the "medieval Greek" rubric to pull off.

In the later period, this picture became inverted and considerably more complex. Millions of ethnic Romans came under Latin or Turkish rule, and so some Greek literature was written under conditions of foreign rule. At the same time, some of those others, including French and Italians in Greece, and Persians in Anatolia, wrote in Greek. Most of this was in a form of Greek that veered toward the vernacular, a register of the language that was also now being used for literary purposes by Romans under their own rulers. I argued above that this corpus can now be called *Romaic*, as it was at the time, and no longer referred to as "quasi-vernacular" Greek (δημώδη). It was written by Romans but also by others too. For instance, the *Chronicle of the Morea* was one of the first long works in Romaic Greek. It issued from the French-Italian colonial outpost in the Peloponnese in the fourteenth century. However, the modern Greek national interpretation of this text struggles to classify it, for, despite its Romaic language, its outlook is pro-French, pro-Catholic, anti-Orthodox, and anti-Roman (though it makes friendly overtures to the ethnic Roman subjects of the western barons in the Peloponnese). It is even harder for the Greek national paradigm to make sense of the Romaic poems of the Persian writers al-Rumi and his son Sultan Walad, who lived in thirteenth-century Anatolia, and so they are rarely mentioned at all. In short, Romaic literature in the late period was not written only by Romans. This is not a case of non-Greek works being written inside Romanía, but of Greek works being written outside it, in other words the inverse of the situation that we observe in the early period.

To be sure, most Greek literature in this period continued to be written by Romans living in the surviving Roman polity, but it was increasingly influenced by literature in other languages, especially Italian and French, and many translations were made into Greek from Latin at the time, as the Romans coped with the rise of western Europe. For this period, scholars of Byzantine literature understand the importance of looking at those other languages too, even if their corpora cannot be incorporated fully into the field, for obvious reasons of practicality. But, as I have been arguing, this cross-cultural approach should be extended to the earlier periods too. An inclusive "east Roman" rubric would work better for this purpose than a "medieval Greek" one. Important developments were taking place in the literary scene of the east Roman world that were not always in Greek.

Many philologists may recoil from this model, given how they understand linguistic expertise and the technical, specialized goals of their research. Surely it will not be possible for any one person to master all these languages to the same degree. That is not, of course, the proposal. The proposal is in fact possibly even more distasteful from the standpoint of the current philological model. It is that the study of east Roman literature will have to move beyond this narrow model and its fixation on technical expertise. Yes, every individual scholar will have to be rooted in one or two of these languages as an expert, but the broader picture will, at some point, have to involve collaboration among experts in different fields. It may even prove necessary to rely on translations to bridge the gap. That is what translations are for, after all. An overarching field of "east Roman literature" will not demand expertise in many languages, but will facilitate dialogue and collaboration among experts in different ones, discussions that are currently not taking place because of academic siloing. There are signs that research might be moving in this direction.[29] "Medieval Greek" will be one contributor to such projects, and will surely remain the most important one, but by itself it will not be able to accomplish this broader goal. Left to its

---

29 E.g., see the collaborative project "Retracing Connections: Byzantine Storyworlds in Greek, Arabic, Georgian, and Old Slavonic (c. 950—c. 1100)" (https://retracingconnections.org).

own devices, there is no indication that it is even inclined to do so. Placing it within a broader paradigm may help to nudge things along.

Even if we limit ourselves to the Greek corpus, which will always be the core of east Roman literature, there is another major reason why the east Roman rubric works better than either a Byzantine or a medieval Greek one. This has to do with the history of Greek literature itself. No new era of Greek literature began in the fourth century, nor did any major developments take place in it at that time, though the vagaries of survival have left us with far more texts from the fourth century than the third. The Byzantine and medieval rubrics imply that something new began then, but that is not the case. The foundation of Constantinople, the adoption of Christianity as the official religion, the separation of the eastern and western halves of the empire, and all the other developments that we associate with the beginnings of Byzantine history hardly impacted the course of Greek literature at that time.[30] All existing genres of writing—including rhetoric, the novel, historiography, epistolography, philosophy, and all Christian literature—continued to develop along stable trajectories that can be traced back to the second century AD. The only new addition was hagiography, though it did not really pick up until the fifth century and it was an extension of ancient biography. Overall, there were no major ruptures in style, language, register, genre, or the social history of reading and writing between the second and sixth centuries.

Therefore, decreeing that "Byzantine" literature begins in the fourth century inappropriately imposes a political periodization on literature. Likewise, "medieval Greek" literature may be said to begin at that time only because it too arbitrarily imposes the alien western concept of the "medieval" on Greek literature, when in reality nothing "medieval"

---

30 Cf. A. Kaldellis, "The Reception of Classical Literature and Ancient Myth," in *Oxford Handbook*, ed. Papaioannou, 162–79, here 162–63.

happened to Greek literature in this period (or even in any period). In sum, this periodization in literature exists only because literature has been forced to align with the a priori category of "Byzantium," which is itself understood as "medieval" in order to please the gods who divided up the modern academic disciplines (ancient vs. medieval, early vs. later Roman empire, pagan vs. Christian, etc.).

One of the advantages of the "east Roman" rubric, which we noted above, is that it is not defined by chronology and so it can reach back into the period of the early empire. Indeed, we *have* to do so in the case of literature because the literary currents that we find in full swing in the fourth century were part of a movement of Greek writing that had begun two centuries earlier. This movement (for lack of a better word) reached, in a relatively coherent form, from the second century down to the early seventh. Its origins lie in Greek Roman authors—or Roman Greek authors—who constituted what classicists conventionally call the Second Sophistic. This produced many authors deemed canonical by later east Romans, including Plutarch, Ailios Aristeides, Hermogenes, Lucian, Galen, and Cassius Dio. This period also saw the origin of Christian apologetics, heresiology, and martyrology, which continued in full swing in the fourth century and beyond. Plutarch wrote the lives of both Greeks and Romans in Greek. Ailios Aristeides wrote orations praising both Athenian culture and the Roman empire. Lucian, whose native language was likely Aramaic, was the first writer of Greek to casually use the first-person plural pronoun in referring to Romans ("we"). In sum, east Roman literature began long before the foundation of Constantinople.

Almost no Greek literature survives from the period immediately before this cluster of writers, that is from before the second century AD, the exceptions being mainly Josephus and the New Testament. That loss, and the exceptions, were no accident. What we have is essentially what later east Romans decided to keep. In other words, the shape of the corpus of surviving ancient Greek literature is, to a significant degree, owed to the choices of later east Romans about which texts to keep and which not.[31] They chose to keep a corpus that ran from those authors of the second century to their successors in the sixth century (with a few stragglers in the seventh). After that, the Arab conquests and the collapse of Romanía led to a decline in the production of literature that lasted until ca. 780. At that point, the tradition reemerged, but reconfigured along somewhat different lines.

In other words, we have an east Roman warrant for treating ca. 150–640 as a coherent phase in the history of Greek literature. For all intents and purposes, we can call it early east Roman literature. The authors mentioned above were for the most part Greek-speaking Roman citizens who were adapting the classical literary tradition to the needs and preferences of an emerging imperial society in the east. This was why they were so appealing to later east Romans and were preserved, whereas most of what had come before them (in the Hellenistic period) was not. There is no good reason to bisect this coherent phase of Greek-Roman imperial literature and posit the emergence of "Byzantine" or "medieval Greek" literature in the fourth century. The only reason this has happened is because other fields—political and religious history—have posited the third or fourth centuries as rupture-points for their own disciplines. To put it bluntly, classicists don't want to read Christian texts, so they stop around 230 AD, and their discipline has a long tradition of disparaging "Byzantine" texts, which are discarded as unworthy on linguistic, literary, and cultural grounds, even though they are written more or less in the same language in which classicists are trained (the prejudice is necessary in this case precisely because the objective differences are so low, indeed virtually non-existent).[32] Meanwhile, historians of the empire have administratively divided it between "early" and "late" phases.

---

31 Cf. A Kaldellis, "The Byzantine Role in the Making of the Corpus of Classical Greek Historiography: A Preliminary Investigation," *Journal of Hellenic Studies* 132 (2012): 71–85.

32 For additional prejudices working against Byzantine literature,

Historians of literature, if they are to respect their archive, should no longer abide by these artificial divisions. We must abolish the distinction between the study of "imperial" literature on the one hand and "late antique" or "early Byzantine" literature on the other. A long east Roman paradigm, beginning in the second century AD, does just that.

Conversely, if Prokopios of Kaisareia (sixth century) was a Byzantine or medieval author, then so were Plutarch and Lucian. If the Christian orators of Gaza (ca. 500) were Byzantine or medieval, then so were the great orators of the second century, such as Ailios Aristeides. The same goes for many other genres of writing that flourished during this movement: collections of lives of learned men; the development of Platonic philosophy and Christian theology; commentaries on Aristotle; manuals of rhetorical theory; Roman history written in Greek; the novel (which also took a Christian form); and others. All this reflected the adaptation of Greek literary culture to the new Roman world in the east. Roman power was also adapting: at the beginning of this period its laws were issued in Latin, but at the end they were in Greek, and this shift took place as part of a gradual evolution, marked by no ruptures. Incidentally, there is no reason for the category "Byzantine law" to even exist. This was just east Roman law, issued first in Latin with Greek translations and then only in Greek.

The study of Byzantine literature will lose nothing by dropping its Byzantine moniker, and it may even gain much. In this section, I have tried to outline what that might be: first, the integration of non-Greek literature into its own social context, which was the same as that of its Greek counterpart; and, second, the reunification of the classicizing movement of Greek literature that began in the second century and paused in the seventh. Finally, we cannot avoid noting that one of the primary associations of the word "Byzantium" is with excessive convolution that creates confusion and is

---

see Agapitos, "Contesting Conceptual Boundaries."

impossible for outsiders to navigate. One expects that per-haps in a tax system, but it gives a terrible first impression for literature.

Periodization

This proposal will likely leave a number of loose ends that will have to be worked out later or by others. One of them is the use of "Byzantine" in periodization, that is to distin-guish among the early, middle, and late Byzantine periods. In the field of Near Eastern archaeology, "Byzantine" by itself is used to refer to the material culture of the fourth-to-seventh centuries. Now, I will be the first to admit that the terms "early east Roman," "middle east Roman," and "late east Roman" would not be elegant and would prove to be unworkable in practice. They would work ok in German, so-so in English, but hardly at all in French and Greek. As adjectives they would look like word piles (e.g., "the middle east Roman armies").

There is another issue regarding periodization, which we should note at the outset. Specifically, the "early Byzantine period" has largely fallen out of use, being employed almost entirely by Byzantinists who work on later periods when they look back. What used to be the early Byzantine period is now called by a wide range of other names, depending on what one is studying. These include the overlapping terms "late Roman," "late antique," "early Christian," "Patristic," and even "early medieval," with the second being probably the most prevalent. These terms are more aspectual than chronological. This tangle looks like a chaotic mess, but it works in practice. One of its consequences is that, for most intents and purposes Byzantium now has only a middle and late period. But it does not have to be that way for east Rome.

One option that we have is to simply leave these terms in place, even the Byzantine ones. This of course presup-poses that our scholarship has been purged entirely of any references to Byzantium and the Byzantines as historical entities. If we manage to do that in our thinking and writing, then perhaps we can retain the period-names as harmless relics of a bygone era. It might not even be necessary to use them often, as in most contexts simply saying "in the middle period" or "in the late period" suffices; for the early period something like "late antique" should also suffice. However, in article and book titles that want to specify a period this would not work, and "Byzantine" would have to be used. To be sure, period-terms in many fields are similarly artificial, e.g., Helladic, Minoan, Geometric, Archaic, and Classical, to use ancient Greece as an example. Perhaps we can still use the old field-name in this minor capacity as a quaint period-marker, provided that we rid it of all ontological commitments to "Byzantium."

But upon further reflection this seems like an unwise choice. It would keep the old Byzantine label active in too many publication titles. But if we don't use Byzantine, and east Roman is too cumbersome for use in some languages, what alternatives do we have? My proposal is to use the period-names "early imperial," "middle imperial," and "late imperial," with no further qualification. There is, to my knowledge, no other field that uses them in this way, so there is no potential for confusion. And the decisive advantage of this system is that it would cover the entire imperial Roman period and imply that it is one unit, even if subdivided into three periods for convenience. Our terminology for the different periods would in fact promote the desirable project of reintegrating Roman imperial history. The early imperial period according to this schema could cover the first six centuries, from Augustus down to the seventh century (and could encompass a subdivision, namely the late antique period for the fourth to the seventh centuries). The viability of this long "early imperial period" as a relatively coherent block of time is being reestablished by recent publications.[33] The middle imperial period would include the next six centuries down to 1204, and the late imperial period would end in the fifteenth

---

33 E.g. O. Hekster, *Caesar Rules: The Emperor in the Changing Roman World (c. 50 BC—AD 565)* (Cambridge: Cambridge University Press, 2023).

century. Dynastic sub-periods (especially the Macedonian, Komnenian, Laskarid, and Palaiologan) could still be used. Meanwhile, Near Eastern archaeologists can easily stop referring to a "Byzantine period," altogether, and call it instead the "late antique" or "late Roman" period (or "late antique Roman").

This solution is simple and elegant. It has one drawback, however, at least for me, though others may be less worried about it. Specifically, it is not clear to me that Romanía actually was an empire during most of its existence.[34] We call states empires for two reasons, sociological and titular. Sociologically, in English (and most modern languages) an "empire" refers to a relation of domination that exists between one ethnic, religious, or political group over a number of others, who have been conquered by it. At times in their history, the east Romans did exercise such domination over others, but this accounted for a minority of the population of their state at any specific time. It certainly wasn't one in its later period. A different sense of "empire" is established via the title of the monarch and its rank status, regardless of the territories and people that he ruled. In this sense too, I am not certain that *basileus* conveyed what the modern languages mean by an "emperor." Perhaps it did in some way, but, strange though it is to say, the field has not yet had this discussion.

Can we use these period-names without prejudging the question of the nature of the east Roman state? I am not sure. In terms of research, this remains an open question, and perhaps we do not want to bias it by the period-names that we adopt, however convenient they may be. I am willing to grant that the east Romans believed that their basileus was in some way superior in status to other kings, or to mere kings, though how exactly this was conceptualized remains murky. Perhaps this convention, relating to the prestige of the ruler rather than the nature of his rule over his subjects, is enough to anchor a system of "imperial" periodization

---

34 Kaldellis, *Romanland*, chap. 6–7.

(early, middle, and late). This system also has the advantage of minimizing, indeed obliterating, any rupture between the early Roman empire and all its later phases, and this advantage outweighs, in my eyes, the debates over "empire" in the later periods.

Conclusions

Byzantine Studies has long resembled a stage that has been flooded by artificial smoke. When you walk onto it, you can discern individual parts of the set if you get up close to them, and see how they are linked to those next to them, but if you try to look at the whole it seems shrouded, opaque, and mysterious. It does not help that we have been pointing colored spotlights at the background too, casting the whole in an unearthly, exotic, and fictionalized light. This is how the concepts "Byzantium" and "the Byzantines" have operated. They rarely prevent scholars from carrying out good research on specialized topics, but when it comes to giving an account of the civilization as a whole, about who its people were, what their relationship was to ancient traditions and their place in world history, the results range from confused or distorted to metaphysical or just made up. The essences that have been invented for Byzantium seem like figures discerned in the clouds.

Getting rid of those labels, along with their accumulated associations, and using instead the labels that are consistently used in our sources will be like a crisp wind blowing the smoke away. We will then be able to see this polity, its society, history, and civilization for what they were, and we will also be able to relate it properly to its antecedents, neighbors, and successors. Our field will no longer be cut off from the mainstream of human history, as a magical land held in the grip of esoteric delusions and mystical essences. It will be as familiar and pedestrian as the Roman empire, which is what it was.

It is imperative that we reclaim the long east Roman paradigm. Byzantine Studies has been losing ground, with its greatest losses going to late antiquity. Late antiquity has occupied a large part of our field and turned it over to classicists and early Christian scholars, who have little inclination to look at anything Byzantine after the seventh century. As a result, Byzantium has never been more cut off from its ancient sources than it is now. It has become a smaller field, more isolated, and Hellenocentric, revolving around Greek sources and the Greek Orthodox Church.

In response to this development, we need to reopen the pathways back to antiquity and reclaim not only what used to be our "early" period, i.e., the late antique east, but also to build bridges back to the early Roman empire. An east Roman paradigm can help to do this, especially if it not constrained by the dates for the foundation of Constantinople and the triumph of Christianity. We need to realize that east Rome as a cultural paradigm was emerging already in the early Roman period. Moreover, an east Roman paradigm can help to integrate the non-Greek traditions that were part of this world, and to resist their segregation along linguistic and confessional lines. The hallmarks of this long east Rome will be integration, bridges between fields, and an openness to the long duration. This will counteract the narrowness and excessive specialization of Byzantium. We need to activate the interest of ancient historians, along with classicists and scholars of Syriac literature and rabbinical studies. This will never happen with a Byzantine paradigm. To wit, it has not.

Revealed as east Rome, as an integral part of Roman history, the society that we study will be better positioned to participate in general debates about history, politics, and society. The Roman experience has always been central to these, at least in western discussions, but Byzantium is either excluded or absent from them, in part because non-experts cannot penetrate the barrier of fantasies and cognitive dissonance that surrounds the very notion of Byzantium. With the mysticism removed from the picture, Romanía can emerge as an integral part of the Roman tradition and thereby join in general discussions of empire, resilience, inequality and meritocracy, sexual politics and gender roles, Church–state relations, religious intolerance, the politics of crowds, the infrastructural capability of premodern states, and many more topics. It will appear as just a later phase of the Roman tradition, hopefully without the stigmas that have attached to it since the era of Montesquieu and Gibbon, or, further back, from the era of the crusades.

An east Roman paradigm will not automatically achieve all this for us, but it will help. It will make what we study not only more real by its own lights and true to its own self-conception, but less strange in the eyes of outsiders, "that weird thing over there with a *y* and a *z* in its name, whose own experts tell us was not what it claimed to be." It would also become more legible to western medieval historians. Medieval Studies is highly invested in the reception of the Roman tradition because it was this, along with the western Church, that gave some coherence to the many cultures of medieval western Europe. But that field has also learned to ignore the eastern empire because of the bias of its own sources and the denialism practiced by our field. We can now push back against that trend and explain all the ways in which the eastern empire contributed to the construction of *western* ideas of Rome, indeed it was fundamental to them, even if its role was suppressed in subsequent memory for precisely the reasons that later generated the dismissive and isolating paradigm of Byzantium. This approach might result in a more interesting and even balanced integration of western and eastern Roman studies. So far attempts to do this have been one-sided, in other words to show how Byzantium was a medieval society on western terms. But what if, at times, the script could be flipped? What if east Rome set the terms that western receptions of Roman culture emulated? East Rome might be able to play this part, but Byzantium already has failed.

We are entering a period of transition between the two paradigms, during which both sets of names will be in use, just like when the euro was introduced and gradually replaced the national currencies. It will take time for the general public to become acquainted with the new shape of things, and that is reasonable. For many scholars too, myself included, the change will require time. Habits of speech acquired long ago and solidified over decades do not change easily. No shaming, calling out, or apologies are necessary. Some may cling to those habits, and that is fine. The change will happen regardless, and it will begin within scholarly practice. Emic terms can more easily hold the high ground, whereas Byzantium is encrusted with bad histories and promotes confusion and isolation. It has failed to ensure a place for east Rome within most models of history, ranging from textbooks and world histories to comparative research projects. Anyone who invokes tradition or mere convention here will be signaling the bankruptcy of our old model and will only hasten its demise. In the end, we will be left with nothing but the name of our institutions—journals, centers, and the like—and these will come to seem archaic, relics of the opacity of politicized fictions. By removing those fictions we will gain something energizing: in the words of a poet-historian of the twelfth century, "a new Rome, forever renewed."[35]

---

35 Konstantinos Manasses, *Historical Synopsis,* 2320–23, ed. O. Lampsidis, *Constantini Manassis Breviarium Chronicum,* 2 vols. (Athens: Academy of Athens, 1996).

Further Reading

For the **history** of the east Roman polity, see A. Kaldellis, *The New Roman Empire: A History of Byzantium* (Oxford: Oxford University Press, 2023). For the **Roman identity** of its population and the tradition of its denial in scholarship, see A. Kaldellis, *Romanland: Ethnicity and Empire in Byzantium* (Cambridge, MA: Harvard University Press, 2019); D. Whalin, *Roman Identity from the Arab Conquests to the Triumph of Orthodoxy* (Cham: Palgrave Macmillan, 2020).

For the history of **early modern scholarship** on Byzantium, and the invention of that name for it, see N. Aschenbrenner and J. Ransohoff, eds., *The Invention of Byzantium in Early Modern Europe* (Washington, DC: Dumbarton Oaks, 2021).

For the history of **western perceptions** of the eastern empire, see the papers in P. Marciniak and Dion C. Smythe, eds., *The Reception of Byzantium in European Culture since 1500* (London: Routledge 2016); and M. Kulhánková and P. Marciniak, eds., *Byzantium in the Popular Imagination: The Modern Reception of the Byzantine Empire* (London: Tauris, 2023).

For a set of stimulating and diverse **critiques of the field** of Byzantine Studies, including the issue of orientalism, see the papers in B. Anderson and M. Ivanova, eds., *Is Byzantine Studies a Colonialist Discipline? Toward a Critical Historiography* (University Park: Penn State University Press, 2023).

For the difficult relationship between Byzantine and **Medieval Studies**, see C. Messis, "Byzance et l'Occident: le cas du *Moyen âge grec* d'Évelyn Patlagean," in *Byzance et l'Europe: l'héritage historioraphique d'Évelyne Patlagean*, ed. C. Delacroix-Besnier (Paris: Centre des études byzantines, EHESS, 2016), 103–18; and A. Kaldellis, *Byzantium Unbound* (Leeds: Arc Humanities Press, 2019), chap. 4.

For **critiques of the concept of the "medieval"** coming from other non-western fields (Indian, Islamic, Japanese, and Chinese), see the papers in the first volume of *The Medieval History Journal* (1998).

For the **colonial conquest** of Romanía by the Fourth Crusade, see G. Demacopoulos, *Colonizing Christianity: Greek and Latin Religious Identity in the Era of the Fourth Crusade* (New York: Fordham University Press, 2019).

For an introduction to **Orthodoxy**, see J. A. McGuckin, *The Orthodox Church: An Introduction to its History, Doctrine, and Spiritual Culture* (Malden: Blackwell, 2010); for Orthodoxy and Byzantine society, see D. Krueger, ed., *Byzantine Christianity* (= *A People's History of Christianity*, vol. 3) (Minneapolis: Fortress, 2006). For the the emperor as the effective head of the Church in the empire, even in matters of doctrine, see P. Heather, *Christendom: The Triumph of a Religion, AD 300–1300* (New York: Knopf, 2023).

For the origins of Byzantine **art history**, see I. Foletti, *From Byzantium to Holy Russia: Nikodim Kondakov (1844–1925) and the Invention of the Icon*, trans. S. Melker (Rome: Viella, 2017); and M. Taroutina, *The Icon and the Square: Russian Modernism and the Russo-Byzantine Revival* (University Park: Penn State University Press, 2018).

For **the debate over east and west** in the origin of Byzantine art, see J. Elsner, "The Birth of Late Antiquity: Riegl and Strzygowski," *Art History* 25 (2002): 358–79; and G. Fowden, *Before and After Muhammad: The First Millennium Refocused* (Princeton: Princeton University Press, 2014), 23–37.

For Byzantine **literature** (as a phase of Greek literature), see S. Papaioannou, ed., *The Oxford Handbook of Byzantine Literature* (Oxford: Oxford University Press, 2021); for late antique literature in all languages, see S. McGill and E. J. Watts, eds., *A Companion to Late Antique Literature* (Hoboken: Blackwell, 2018); for some of the problems caused by the taxonomies into which Byzantine literature has been placed, see P. Agapitos, "Contesting Conceptual Boundaries: Byzantine Literature and its History," *Interfaces: A Journal of Medieval European Literatures* 1 (2015): 62–91.

Printed and bound by CPI Group (UK) Ltd, Croydon, CR0 4YY

13/04/2025

14656453-0001